W9-BIE-442

HOW DO YOU SURVIVE A DUEL?

To Ellen, Cathy and Les, who provide tranquility and comfort.

Published by SevenOaks in 2018
an imprint of Carlton Books Ltd
20 Mortimer Street
London W1T 3JW

A catalogue record for this book is available from the British Library

ISBN 978-1-78177-800-5

Printed in Dubai

10 9 8 7 6 5 4 3 2 1

Author's acknowledgement:
To Victor Serebriakoff, Professor Hans Eysenck, Scot Morris, Eamonn Butler and Madson Pirie, for permission to use some material from their works.

The material in this book was previously published as *World Class Puzzles*.

HOW DO YOU SURVIVE A DUEL?

AND OTHER MATHEMATICAL DIVERSIONS, PUZZLES AND BRAINTEASERS

ERWIN BRECHER

SEVENOAKS

CONTENTS

INTRODUCTION

We are told that regular exercise is one of the most important contributions to health and physical well-being. Jogging will tone your muscles, but what does it do for your brain? Mental fitness is equally important, and the way you achieve it is to become a problem-solver. You will soon enjoy the exercise, and you will be rewarded with a profound sense of achievement with every puzzle you crack.

In this book I have assembled a wide and varied array of problems to tax the mind and offer intellectual stimulus to even seasoned puzzle enthusiasts who might think that they have seen it all before.

Incidentally, many so-called brain-teasers are nothing of the sort; often nothing more than mathematical textbook exercises that can be solved using simple quations or geometrical formulae. As such, these are not much of a challenge to a reader's problem-solving faculties. In my selection precess, therefore, I have concentrated on material that requires a great deal of inspirational thinking but a minimum of mathematical expertise, catering in part to the many puzzle fans who have an inborn aversion to all thing mathematical.

I have overcome an aversion to trick questions, previously enunciated elsewhere. Deemed inappropriate for another work, which included so esoteric a subject as "The Fourth Dimension", here I see them as apposite and a challenge to the alert and quick-witted mind.

In books, too, I have tended to exclude other types of puzzles, such as "river crossings" and "liars and truth-tellers", so often found in puzzle literature. To my mind, the former is essentially a somewhat tedious trial-and-error exercise, while the latter uses one single basic idea in what becomes monotonous variations. Here, however, you are offered a soupçon, a taste, of "liars" to start you off.

To repeat, preference has been given to puzzles that make demands on the reader's reasoning facilities rather than on dimly remembered mathematical operations. Many can be solved both ways, and some readers might derived satisfaction from finding the equation that will confirm the solution found by reasoning or trial-and-error.

I have also introduced material on probabilities and permutations. Many of you might consider this a somewhat arcane subject, but if you persevere you will soon get into the swing of it and enjoy the perfplexing and contradictory solutions which fallacious thinking can produce.

If this book does nothing more than give your mind's muscles a good workout, it will have achieved its purpose.

Erwin Brecher

GENERAL PUZZLES

1. LIARS AND TRUTH-TELLERS I

Fred and Harry are two friends who have much in common except that one of them always tells the truth and the other always lies.

Formulate a question, to be asked of only one of them, to which the answer will be "No" regardless of whether you ask Fred or Harry.

2. LIARS AND TRUTH-TELLERS II

Building on the above, what question would you have to ask either Fred or Harry to establish who is who, liar or truth-teller?

3. ANOTHER LIARS AND TRUTH-TELLERS

On one of your trips around the world you meet three tribesmen called Ching, Chang and Chung. The remarkable trait of their tribal community is that each member consistently either lies or tells the truth. You first address Ching and ask him to which sect he belongs. Ching does not speak English, but he is able to make out your question and he replies in his native tongue, which you, in turn, don't understand. Chang tries to be helpful and intervenes, saying, "Ching said that he is a liar." Chung seems upset, and tells you in impeccable English, "Don't believe Chang, he is a liar."

Question: Who is who, liar or truth-teller?

(NOTE: If after these three examples you, notwithstanding my reservations, find this type of puzzle intriguing, try constructing your own liars-and-truth-tellers puzzles to amuse friends.)

4. SIBLINGS

"Listen, Fred," Steve said to his friend, "work this one out. I have twice as many sisters as I have brothers, while my sister Joanna has as many sisters as brothers. How many boys and girls are we?"

"That's easy," responded Fred, "but now it's your turn. I have three times as many sisters as brothers, while any of my sisters has the same number of sisters and brothers."

A. How many sisters and brothers are there in Steve's family?
B. How many sisters and brothers are there in Fred's family?

5. THE BRIDGE PARTY

During a high-stakes bridge competition preceded by a sit-down dinner, Dick, Tom, Harry and Fred played together. At the end of the evening, all four had more cash than when they had arrived. In other words, none of them lost although they were playing for money. How could this be?

6. GOLDEN WEDDING

Oscar and Marianne invited their large family to a special anniversary gathering to be held at the Dorchester Hotel. They came bearing presents and, of course, a good time was had by all. There was daughter Yvonne, the son Mark, his sister-in-law, Auntie Selma, Uncle Tom, and his son William. There was Selma's stepson with his cousin and, last but not least, Oscar's sister.

In this list one guest stands out. Who is it?

7. THE ENCYCLOPEDIA

David, Danny and George had a total of 60 one-pound coins in their pockets.

They wanted to buy a puzzle encyclopedia which was, however, priced at £72. In desperation, they looked up another pal, Henry, and asked him whether he had enough money to make up the difference.

Henry smiled and jingled some coins in his pocket.

"As you seem to be interested in puzzles, I will contribute only if you can guess how many one-pound coins I have. The only clue I will give you is this: I have three coins fewer than the average number of coins in our four pockets." How many coins did Henry have?

8. SECOND TIME AROUND

For both Ellen and Richard it was the second attempt at happiness. They had each been married before and, when they exchanged rings, each of them had children of their own. Still, they both loved children so, many years later, their offspring had grown to fourteen, more than enough to man a football team. Each parent was related by blood to ten of their children.

How many were born to Ellen and Richard?

9. CLUB 54

When Carla tried to enter Club 54's premises, the doorman pointed to a posted notice: "Admittance restricted to guests 17 years of age or older." "If I prove to you," Carla retorted, "that in three years I will be one and a half times as old as I was four years ago, will you let me in?" John, the doorman, being a member of Mensa, thought for only a few moments before making his decision.

Did Carla qualify?

10. A BOTTLE OF WINE

Here you have a balance scale that is in equilibrium, with three bottles of wine on one side and another bottle of the same wine plus three bars of 24-carat gold, weighing ½ kg. each, on the other side.

How much does each bottle of wine weigh?

11. PENCIL PAPER AND LOGIC

If a third of twenty were eight, how much would ten be?

This sounds confusing, but with pencil, paper and a little logic you will make short shrift of it

12. JOE'S HIDEAWAY

Joe serves a set dinner for £20. In order to promote business, he introduces a program offering one free meal for every six dinners paid.

Would it be cheaper for Fred to take six friends out to dinner once or two guests out to dinner twice?

13. THE MONTE CARLO RALLY

Stephen Roberts was driving his Maserati for the 1,200-kilometre course. He had bought six new Michelin balloon tyres, including two spares. For testing purposes he intended to expose each tyre to the same distance.

What was this distance?

14. NEXT LETTER

What is the next letter in this sequence?

D N O S A J J M A ?

15. THE TEST

Three applicants, Dick, Tom and Harry, applied for the position of chief executive in Intertrust Ltd. To test their intelligence and reasoning powers, the chairman showed them five discs of which two were white and three red. He then attached, unseen by any of them, one red disc to the back of each applicant and palmed the white disc. Finally, he explained that the applicant who first announced the colour of his own disc correctly, and could explain his reasoning, would get the job. Dick, having looked at the red discs on the backs of Tom and Harry, stepped forward after a few moments' thought and stated that his disc was red.

What was his reasoning?

16. THE GAMBLERS

On another occasion, Tom and Dick were joined by their friend Harry. They passed a middle-aged beggar sitting on a newspaper with an empty whisky bottle by his side. "He can't be all that hard up," thought Tom and, seizing a betting opportunity, he turned to his friends: "I bet each of you a fiver that this fellow has more than £10 in his pocket" "Done," said Dick. "I bet the same amount that he has less than £10." Harry, not wanting to be left out, said, "I bet both of you that he has more than £1 in his pocket".

If only one of the three friends could claim to have won the bet, how much money did the beggar have on him?

17. THE BARGAIN

Leo was selling expensive Swiss Piaget watches from his stall in Petticoat Lane at knockdown prices. Some suspicious minds might have whispered that they must have fallen off the back of a passing lorry, or truck; others had visions of money changing hands in shadowy exotic locales.

Although Leo's persuasive spiel, spiced as it was with humour, drew crowds, sales remained sluggish. His price for each watch was £22, but finally, as it looked like rain and Leo wanted to get a move on, he changed his marketing strategy and offered two watches for £36. This helped to clear the lot out quickly but, while packing up, he shook his head over the fact that, by selling the two at the bargain price, he had made only £1 on the second watch.

How much had he paid for the watches?

18. TRYING TO ESCAPE

George (Tiny) Williams and Alfie (Slim) Watson were serving five-year stretches for robbery. They got their nicknames because George stood six foot four, and Alfie, though only five foot seven in height, weighed as much as George.

They had been preparing their escape for several months and were satisfied that, in its simplicity, it was bound to work. They had managed to steal a two-metre rope from the workshop. All they had to do was fix one end to the steel railing on top of the prison wall.

One night, carefully dodging the searchlights, they both reached the wall. Alfie climbed onto George's shoulders with the rope in his hand. To their disappointment, no matter how much Alfie stretched, he was two inches too short to reach the railing, and they had to abandon their attempt.

It appears that the two had more brawn than brains. Could they have done better?

19. THE LAWN

Adam, Danny and Fred wanted to surprise their parents, who were away on a long weekend, by mowing the large lawn at the back of their house. Adam, working alone, would need twelve hours. Danny could do it in six hours, but Fred would need only four hours.

How long would it take to finish the job if the three brothers joined forces, working together?

20. SECOND AND THIRD

The object I have in mind is the third of its kind, yet strangely enough it is always referred to as the second of its kind.

What is it?

21. GUESSING THE ODDS

You and George are waiting for two friends to make up a game of bridge. To while away the time, you are facing George across the table and each of you has a well-shuffled pack of cards (52) in front of you. Each of you turns over one card at a time.

What do you estimate the odds are that two cards turned over together are the same?

22. THE LONG DIVISION

Solve the following sequence of divisions:

What is one-half of two-thirds of three-quarters of four-fifths of five-sixths of six-sevenths of seven-eighths of eight-ninths of nine-tenths of one hundred?

To find the solution without getting tied up in knots, you need a flash of inspiration.

23. A STRANGE PRICING POLICY

Our local stationery and office equipment store held its fourth sale of the year. I am always one for a bargain but, after looking at the merchandise offered, the store's pricing policy did not seem to make much sense. I found the following items on display:

Portable typewriter	£18
Calculator	£10
Ring file	£8
Thesaurus	£9
Dictionary	£10

So far so good. But when I came, next, to a personal computer selling for only £16, I thought someone had omitted two zeros.

Can you explain how the store priced the merchandise?

24. THE SURVEY

A local survey produced the following population breakdown:

60% were female
70% of the population had blue eyes
80% had blond hair

What is the smallest female percentage of the population with blue eyes and blond hair?

25. HEART AND ARROW

When Gloria was eight she developed a crush on Egon, the boy next door, who was eighteen. To give her hope, he carved a heart with an arrow into a cherry tree. The love sign was out of Gloria's reach by 16 centimetres. Egon promised to marry her when she was tall enough to carve her initials next to his.

If Gloria's reach increased by 8 centimetres a year, while the tree was growing by 7 centimetres each year, how old was Gloria when she could ask Egon to keep his promise?

26. DIVIDE AND MULTIPLY

Divide 60 by $^1/_2$, multiply by $^1/_3$, and add 20. What is the result?

27. CLIMBING THE MATTERHORN

Fred and Harry were about to fulfill their lifelong ambition. Starting from the base camp, Fred carried the heavy equipment for the first four kilometres, and Harry took over for the rest of the climb to the peak. On the way back, taking the same route, Fred started off, and Harry carried the load for the last five kilometres to the base.

Which of the climbers carried the equipment farther and by how much?

28. UNUSUAL FRACTIONS

The symbol ∞ stands for infinity and refers to an unlimited quantum which is greater than any fixed amount.

0, the symbol for zero, indicates an absence of quantity or magnitude.

Now solve the following fractions using simple logic:

A.	$\frac{1}{\infty}$	=	?	D.	$\frac{\infty}{\infty}$	=	?
B.	$\frac{1}{0}$	=	?	E.	$\frac{0}{\infty}$	=	?
C.	$\frac{\infty}{0}$	=	?	F.	$\frac{0}{0}$	=	?

29. A HEAVY SMOKER

A man smoked one hundred and twenty cigarettes in five days, each day smoking six more than on the previous day.

How many cigarettes did he smoke on the first day?

30. RELATION

What is the closest relation that my mother's brother-in-law's sister-in-law could be to me?

31. THE WATER-SKIER

Sonny loves his sport. Unfortunately, the only waterway near his home is a stream. Skiing down the river, he can cover the three kilometres to his friend's waterside cabin in six minutes. Returning the same distance upstream takes twelve minutes.

Sonny wonders how long it would take him to cover the same three kilometres on a lake, assuming that the speedboat uses the same power throughout. Can you help him?

32. THE HUNGRY HUNTER

A hunter, having run out of food, met two shepherds. One of them had three loaves of bread, and the other shepherd had five identical loaves. When the hunter asked for sustenance, the shepherds decided to divide the loaves equally among the three of them. The hunter thanked them profusely and gave them eight pounds.

How should the shepherds divide the money?

33. THE LONELY FLIGHT

A lone pilot flies for 420 miles precisely due north, and then changes direction and flies precisely due south for 400 miles.

What is the shortest and longest distance he could be from the point of takeoff to the point of landing?

34. POOL RESOURCES

Brothers Andrew and Jim had just received their weekly pocket money, and planned to go the fairground for the afternoon. Suspecting a smaller allowance, Jim suggested to Andrew that they should pool and share their cash equally. "OK," said Andrew, "I know how much you have. If you can guess how much I have, I will split it with you. To help you, here is a clue:

"If you give me a one-pound coin, I shall have twice as much as you; if instead I give you a pound, we shall each have the same amount."

How much pocket money has each of the brothers received?

35. ADD AND MULTIPLY

What number gives the same result when added to $1^1/_2$ as when it is multiplied by $1^1/_2$? This can be solved by trial and error, but also by a very simple equation.

36. CATCHING THE TRAIN

John's watch is five minutes fast but he believes it is ten minutes slow. Fred's watch is ten minutes slow but he thinks it is five minutes fast.

They both plan to catch the 12 o'clock train to Glasgow. Who will get to the station first?

37. TELL THE TIME

Henry is a puzzle enthusiast, though his addiction is not always shared by his friend Bill. They arranged to meet at the Café Royal, and when Bill asked Henry to suggest a time this is what his friend proposed: "Assume that three hours before we meet was as long after 3 a.m. as it was before 3 p.m., and that answers your question."

Bill, in spite of his aversion to puzzles, was on time. Would you have been?

38. THE NEXT NUMBER

What number comes next?

1 4 7 11 15 19 ?

Clues:

1. It is smaller than nineteen.
2. You will look in vain for a numerical series.

39. FIND THE WORD

Find the word in the second line which fits best in the first

All Board Cast Charge Land Rate

Vision Future Sight Smell Taste Touch

40. THE SWISS SMUGGLERS

Titus and Margaret were driving from Geneva to London using the Channel Tunnel for the first time. Titus had thirty cartons of cigarettes and Margaret twenty cartons hidden under the back seat, hoping to evade duty and tax.

They were caught in a random check and had to pay tax without allowances on exempt quantities. Being short of cash, Titus paid £144 and settled the balance by surrendering twelve cartons. Margaret, not wanting to break open a case, and needing the money, also parted with twelve cartons, and received £96 in change.

Assuming that the customs officer accepted the cigarettes in payment at cost, what was the duty payable and how much did a carton cost?

41. THE THREE DIGITS

Find the three digits in the empty bracket on the second line that follow the same principle as 444 in the bracket in the line above.

128 (444) 316
118 (_ _ _) 382

42. ANALOGY

If 5 were –8, how much would –10 be?

43. EARLY BURIAL

A man was killed during a vicious fight in 1958, and was buried in 1957. Explain.

44. THE AUCTION

I bought a set of wine glasses at an auction. When I came home I discovered that two-thirds of them were scratched, half were chipped, a quarter were both scratched and chipped, and only one was in pristine condition.

How many glasses were in the set I bought?

45. THE GOLD COIN

My friend Charles was a keen collector of antique coins. I happened to come across one of the rare 20-cent pieces minted in gold in the United States during the eighteenth century. I intended to give it to him as a birthday present provided he could solve a little puzzle.

"Here are three boxes," I told him, "marked A, B and C, with the following labels:

A 1. The coin is not in here.
  2. The coin was minted in 1750.
B 1. The coin is not in the box marked A.
  2. It was minted in 1799.
C 1. The coin is not in this box.
  2. The coin is in the box marked B."

I challenged Charles to find the 20-cent gold piece on the understanding that no label contained more than one false statement. Can you do it?

46. STRANGE SYMBOLS

In a row, an explorer comes across the symbols below.

Although the line seems to continue, he cannot make out the next two symbols following. Can you help him?

47. THE PIGGY BANK

After having saved fifty pence coins for three years, Henry dropped his piggy bank "accidentally," breaking it open and scattering a large number of coins all over the floor. Henry picked up a handful while his brother James pocketed three times as many. Thereafter, the following trading took place:

1. Henry gave James six coins.
2. James returned to Henry three times as many as Henry had left.

How many coins was James left with?

48. NEW YEAR'S EVE

For his fortieth birthday last year, Bert was presented with a photograph album covering most of his life.

When he came to a photograph taken during a New Year celebration, showing an old man representing the past year and Bert dressed as a little angel with a crown with the New Year in gold numbers on it, he had to smile. By mistake, his mother had sewn the number the wrong way up, and yet no one had noticed.

How come?

49. THE CHANNEL TUNNEL

The Eurostar travels from London to Paris at 190 kilometres per hour. The French TGV leaves Paris at the same time and travels at 200 kilometres per hour. If both trips are non-stop, how far apart are the trains 40 minutes before they meet?

50. THE DELIVERY

Samson Ltd. are contracted to deliver a load of computers from their warehouse to a customer's head office precisely at noon. If their lorry travelled at 60 miles per hour it would arrive at 11 a.m. — an hour too early. Travelling at 30 miles per hour, the estimated time of arrival would be 1 p.m. — an hour too late.

1. How far is the customer's head office from Samson's warehouse?
2. At what constant speed should the lorry travel to arrive at the destination at noon precisely?

51. THE CROWDED TRAIN

The train to Torquay was crowded, so Joe had to stand in the corridor until exactly halfway to his destination. One passenger then alighted, and Joe quickly sat down. As it happened, when he had half as far to go as he had been sitting, an elderly lady boarded the train. Gentleman that he was, Joe offered her his seat. When the train pulled into Torquay, Joe tried to work out the proportion of the journey during which he had been standing. What was it?

52. THE RACE

Along a straight road there are ten telegraph poles with equal distances of 1 kilometre between them. Fred and Ernest decide to race, both starting from the first pole. Fred, who can run at a steady 10 kilometres per hour, is to turn round at the fifth pole, without losing any time, and run back to the first pole. Ernest, who is faster, at 11 kilometres per hour, is to run to the tenth pole.

Would both arrive at their destinations at the same time? If not, who would be first?

53. RELATIONSHIP

What is the closest relation the son of your father's brother's sister-in-law could be to you?

54. THE FRACTION

Take a fraction such as $^1/_5$. If you add its denominator, the 5, to both the top and bottom of the fraction, you get:

$$\frac{1+5}{5+5} = \frac{6}{10}$$

This construct then reduces to three-fifths, and you have tripled the original fraction.

Now find a fraction which will quadruple in value if you add its denominator to its numerator and denominator.

55. CHRISTMAS SHOPPING

Margaret, Joan and Sheila go Christmas shopping to buy presents. All the boxes are the same size and wrapped in the same paper. At the checkout, the parcels get mixed up. What is the probability that:

1. At least one of the ladies gets the present she bought?
2. Only one lady gets a wrong present?

56. DECK OF CARDS

Take a pack consisting of 52 cards. Divide it at random into two lots (L1 and L2). If a card is pulled from L1, the odds are 3 to 1 that it is a black card. If four red cards are transferred from L1 to L2 and subsequently a card is drawn from L2, the odds are 3 to 1 that a red card appears.

How was the deck originally divided?

57. THREE CARDS

The values attached to a deck of bridge cards start with the Two of Clubs as the lowest, with Diamonds, Hearts and the Ace of Spades as the highest.

If you draw three cards at random from the deck, what is the probability that they will be drawn in order of increasing value?

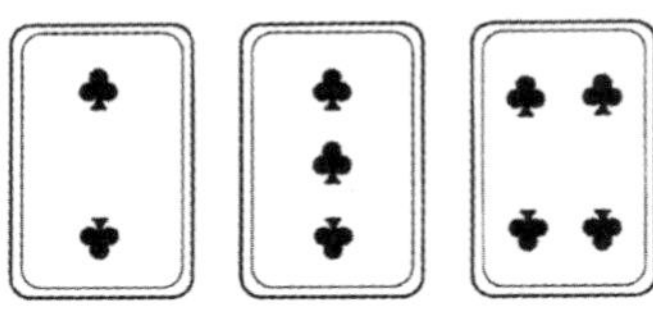

58. YOUR VERY OWN

What belongs to you alone, but is mostly used by others?

59. THE CONFERENCE

Globus Plc held their annual conference at the Grand Hotel in Brighton. Of the one hundred people present:

60 were men
70 were non-smokers
80 were married
90 were from London

What is the least number of married men who were non-smokers and living in London?

60. A FAMILY PUZZLE

Elsa, Jenny, Tom and Harry were sitting around having tea together. Suddenly Jenny interrupted the usual small talk: "Do you realize, Tom, that Elsa is the same relation to you as I am to Harry?" "True, true," responded Tom, "and you are the same relation to me as Elsa is to you."

What were their relationships?

61. GUESS THE NUMBER

I have written down a fraction which I want you to find. Your only clue is: $^5/_9$ is $^2/_3$ of it.

What is the fraction?

62. THE STABLE

Dick, Tom and Harry came to old Sam's stable. "We want to hire some horses for a ride. How many do you have?" Sam, in no mood to be civil, responded: "Work it out for yourselves. I have three-quarters of the number of horses plus three-quarters of a horse."

How many horses did Sam have?

63. THE PUNCTURE

Brian is driving to the seaside in his new Ford Fiesta. After going two-thirds of the way he suffers a puncture and has to abandon his car. Fortunately, he has a bicycle with him, so he can continue his journey. This takes him, however, three times as long as it would have driving the Fiesta.

How many times faster is the car?

64. THE DOLE

After the closure of a textile factory in a small Lancashire town, one third of the men drew unemployment benefits of £45 per week and one half of the women £30 per week. A total of £15,000 was paid out

What was the total population of the town?

65. THE DISTANCE RUNNERS

Stephen and Charles are starting from point A. Their destination is point B, ten miles away. Stephen runs half the time and walks the second half. Charles runs halfway and then walks the remaining five miles.

1. Who would reach B first, assuming that they both run and walk at the same speed?
2. Suppose they walked first and then ran. Would that make any difference?

66. TWO WALL CLOCKS

My kitchen clock is one second fast each hour. My father's bathroom clock loses one and a half seconds per hour. It so happened that they both showed 11 a.m. this morning.

1. When will they show the same time again at any time during the day?
2. When will both clocks show the correct time?

67. THE APPLICANTS

Two men, Andrew and David, apply for the same position, one that offers excellent prospects but requires a great deal of problem-solving ability. Both of their CVs make good reading, and surprisingly they both pass an IQ test with the identical score of 132.

To decide who is the better man, Jonathan Roberts, the chief executive interviewing them, proposes the following test:

"I have three hats, two white and one black. I shall keep one in the drawer, switch off the light and put one hat on each of your heads. The room is in complete darkness, with no mirrors. I will then switch on the light, and whoever guesses the colour of the hat he is wearing will get the job."

Three seconds after the lights came on, Andrew raises his arm and pronounces the colour of his hat.

How did he know, and what was the colour?

68. THE PICNIC

Tom and Mary decided to have a picnic. Mary brought the wine and Tom the sandwiches, which cost only a quarter the price of the wine. Sitting in the park, they were just about to unpack the goodies when their friend Jonathan came along with a hungry look on his face. "OK," said Tom, "we share everything alike, but you have to give us £5 to pay your fair share."

How much did the wine cost?

69. BALANCE THE SCALE

How many triangles will balance the fourth scale?

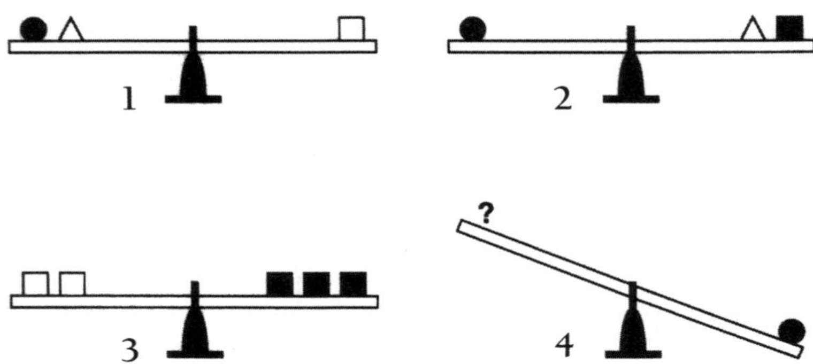

70. THE COUNTERFEIT COIN

Paying for a magazine with a £10 note, I received nine £1 coins in change. Later, the newsagent phoned to tell me that one of the coins was a fake, slightly under weight but otherwise indistinguishable from the real thing.

What is the minimum number of weighings, using a two-pan scale, necessary to locate the counterfeit coin?

71. THE WHIPLASH

When a circus performer working with lions uses his whip, you will hear a sharp, cracking noise. What causes it?

72. HIDE AND SEEK

Tony and Evelyne are playing in the park. Tony counts to twenty and Evelyne hides behind a nearby tree. Tony suspects the tree but, as he circles it, Evelyne keeps the tree between herself and Tony.

The question is: Does Tony not only circle the tree but walk around Evelyne as well?

73. THE WALK TO MARBELLA

Allen, staying at the Hotel Los Monteros on Spain's Costa del Sol, decided to walk the five miles to Marbella. He walked at a steady two miles per hour. When he reached Marbella, he had counted forty buses which overtook him, while fifty buses had passed coming from Marbella.

What was the average speed of the buses?

74. DROPPING A BRICK

We know from Galileo that, ignoring air resistance, all bodies fall with the same acceleration. But how is it with bodies sinking in water of different temperatures?

Suppose you drop a brick in each of two identical vessels, one filled with water at 30° C. and the other at 30° F. Which brick, if any, would sink faster?

75. THE BRIDGE

The bridge over the Danube at Passau, Germany, was declared unsafe and scheduled for demolition. Before being closed to traffic, vehicles were allowed to cross only if their weight did not exceed 5,000 kilograms (11,000 pounds), as any weight over that amount, no matter how small, could cause the bridge to collapse.

A lorry belonging to Unitex Corporation had a load of copper ingots to deliver. The weighbridge indicated 5,200 kilograms, and the driver had to unload several ingots to get down to exactly the maximum permitted weight.

The lorry was almost across the bridge when a pigeon landed on top of it. The bridge did not collapse. Why not?

76. SHATTER A WINE GLASS

Soprano Maria Callas is said to have entertained guests on Onnasis's yacht with her ability to shatter wine glasses by singing a certain note at a high pitch. What happens to the glass, and why does the note have to be sustained?

77. WHAT'S THE TIME?

Four hours ago, it was as long after 4 a.m. as it was before 4 p.m. the same day. What time is it now?

78. DECIPHER THE CODE

The message below is written in code. Break the code and read the message. (Give this some thought and you should find a clue which will help you.)

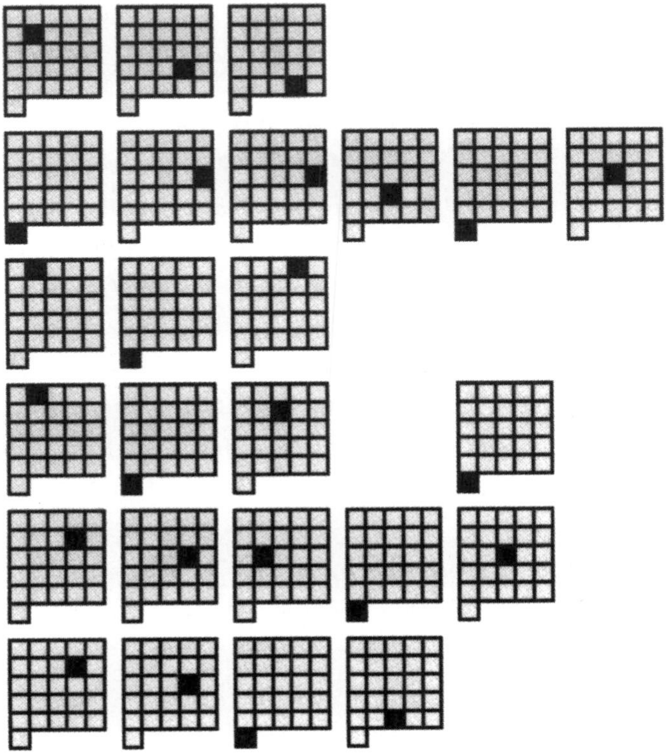

79. THE PARTY

You are attending a cocktail party with your favourite girlfriend. Strangely enough, there is something in the room which everybody can touch, and so can you, but only with your left hand.

How come?

80. THE I.Q. TESTS

In the city of Shrewsbury, there are three schools for bright students. However, the headmasters of the classes for age group 13–14 were not satisfied with the average IQ scores achieved by their students.

One of the headmasters, after reading a book entitled *The IQ Booster,* suggested that the schools hire a psychometrician to try to raise the IQ test performance of their classes. Professor Sudsic answered the ad and the following terms were agreed upon: If he failed to raise the average IQ score of each class within a month, there would be no charge. If he succeeded, however, he would receive a £5,000 bonus.

After three days, he proved to the headmasters that he had succeeded. The schools paid as agreed, but felt cheated. Why?

81. A NUMBER RIDDLE

There are two columns of numbers below.

Can you make the two columns add up to the same total by only moving one disk and not removing any?

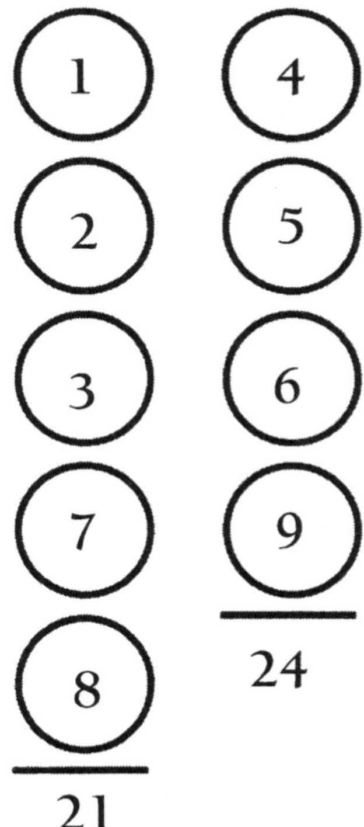

82. THE STEEL PLATE

Fred and Harry were asked to deliver a heavy steel plate to a rolling mill, a distance of exactly 200 metres. They found two empty drums, both with a circumference of 2 metres, and decided to roll the plate instead of carrying it. It wasn't easy, as one had to balance the plate as it rolled off one barrel, which then had to be moved to the front.

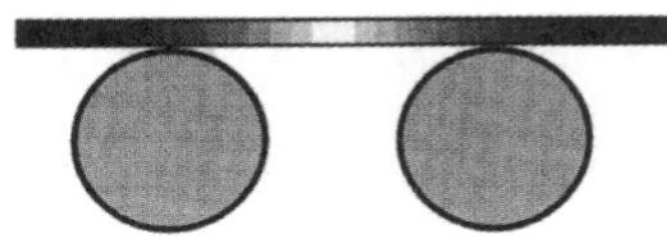

How many revolutions will the drums have completed in order to transport the plate 100 metres?

83. COMPLETE THE SET

Which letter belongs in the empty circle to complete the set?

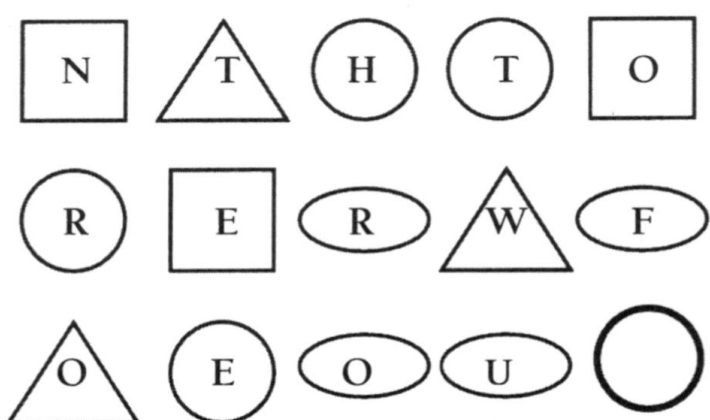

84. THE DATE

Hugo and Lynn were compatible in all respects but one: Hugo was a stickler for being punctual while Lynn was always late.

One day they went their separate ways while shopping but arranged to meet at 5 p.m. in front of the Odeon Theatre in Leicester Square. Hugo had warned Lynn that he would wait a quarter of an hour, but not a minute more.

As the time approached, Hugo found that his watch had stopped. He asked a policeman for the correct time. The policeman's watch was ten minutes fast, but he thought that it was fifteen minutes slow and, in his answer, gave the time he thought was correct. Lynn, in turn, had forgotten her watch. She asked a postman for the time. His watch was ten minutes slow, but he thought that it was fifteen minutes fast.

Considering that both Hugo and Lynn got wrong information, what time would each arrive at the Odeon?

85. THE RECIPE

To bake a cake, you need precisely three-quarters of a glass of milk. Unfortunately, the glass is currently full of milk, and you have no scales, no measuring instruments, and the glass has no marked measurements. All you have is a roll of adhesive tape.

How do you obtain the required quantity of milk for the cake recipe?

86. GEARS

Five gears are in constant mesh, as shown:

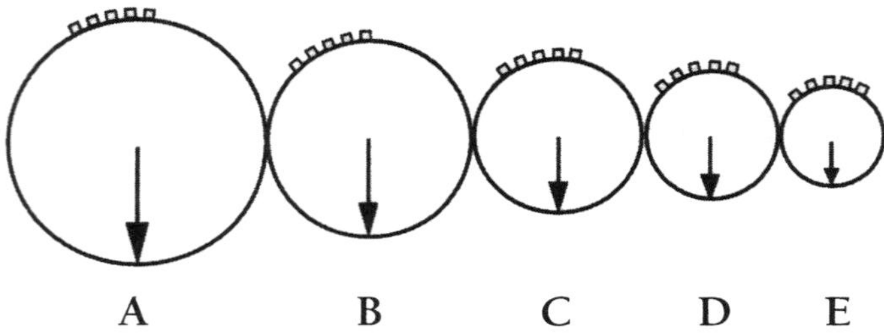

The gears have the following numbers of teeth:

A	116
B	56
C	32
D	20
E	10

As A starts rotating, all the other gears will revolve. How many revolutions will gear C have to make before all the arrows point down again for the first time?

87. STRANGE SITUATION

Two Japanese who have never seen each other meet at the Japanese Embassy in New York and decide to have drinks together in a nearby bar. Incidentally, one is the father of the other one's son.

How is this possible?

88. AMBIGUOUS

All but one of the following words require clarification as to their precise meaning. Which is the odd word out, and why?

Suspect Dive Race Taste Borrow Drive

89. CARD GAMES

I have three friends who love playing cards. Two play rummy, two play bridge, and two play poker. The one who does not play poker also does not play rummy. The one who does not play rummy does not play bridge either.

Which game is played by each friend?

90. THE JEWELLERY SHOP

Martin Green was getting on in age. At 70 he was still active in his small store located in a side street off Harrow Road, selling inexpensive trinkets, rings and similar low-priced merchandise. His lease would run out in three years' time, and he would then finally retire, with modest profits augmenting his small pension to make him feel financially comfortable.

His concern at the moment was repeated daytime robberies. In fact, young hoodlums had just walked in, taken the day's receipts and some odd pieces of jewellery, and left unhurriedly. There was not much that Martin could do, and the police showed little interest. The loss was his own, as he could not afford the premium for adequate insurance coverage. Yet, although Martin Green was old and frail, he was smart He soon found a solution that stopped the robberies at his shop for good.

What did the shopkeeper do?

91. IDIOT SAVANT

French for "knowledgeable idiot", you might have heard of this phenomenon which describes an individual who has an extremely low IQ rating yet nevertheless possesses some extraordinary talent, such as a computer-like ability to perform fairly complicated arithmetical calculations at high speed.

Can you match their aptitude by adding the column of numbers below in 20 seconds?

125,419
113,141
123,456
151,627
152,637
147,363
148,373
176,544
186,859
174,581

?

92. THE BOARD MEETING

"Here are the management accounts and the chairman's report," Jeffrey, the CEO, said to his secretary. "Please copy and distribute, keeping one set for the file." Susan photocopied 169 sheets of paper. How many directors (excluding the chairman) attended the meeting?

93. THE PC PROBLEM

Dear Steve,

Because of a problem with my PC, it took me longer than it should have to write this letter. If you cam decipher the last paragraph you will be pleasantly surprised. To help you, this letter contains a clue.

Og upi dpzbr oy. upi vsm lrra yjr AV O zrmy upi/

Nrdy trhstfd

Fsbof

94. THE LARGE FAMILY

The Grahams were blessed with a large family. They had three daughters, three sons and eighteen grandchildren. Ed, one of the sons, was taking a stroll with his sister Angela. As they were passing a particular house, Ed said, "I want to drop in and say hello to Lisa, my niece. Are you coming with me?"

"No, since I have no niece," replied Angela with a wry smile.

How is this possible?

95. A PAIR OF SOCKS

Inside the drawer of a dressing-table in a dark room, there are 28 black socks and 28 brown socks. What is the minimum number of socks that I must take out of the drawer to guarantee that I have a matching pair?

96. HAIR

Given that there are more people living in Dublin than there are hairs on the head of any Dubliner, and that no Dubliner is totally bald, does it necessarily follow that there must be at least two Dubliners with exactly the same number of hairs?

On the island of Alopecia the following facts are true:

1. No two islanders have exactly the same number of hairs.
2. No islander has precisely 450 hairs.
3. There are more islanders than there are hairs on the head of any one islander.

What is the largest possible number of islanders on Alopecia?

97. THE CLOCK-WATCHER

George did not have a wristwatch, but he did have an accurate clock. However, he sometimes forgot to wind his clock. Once when this happened, George went to his sister's house, spent the evening with her, went back home and set his clock. How could he do this without knowing beforehand the length of the trip?

98. THE PRISONERS' TEST

A wicked king amuses himself by putting 3 prisoners to a test. He takes 3 hats from a box containing 5 hats—3 red hats and 2 white hats. He puts one hat on each prisoner, leaving the remaining hats in the box. He informs the men of the total number of hats of each colour, then says, "I want you men to try to determine the colour of the hat on your own head. The first man who does so correctly, and can explain his reasoning, will immediately be set free. But if any of you answers incorrectly, you will be executed on the spot."

The first man looks at the other two, and says, "I don't know."

The second man looks at the hats on the first and third man, and finally says, "I don't know the colour of my hat, either."

The third man is at something of a disadvantage. He is blind. But he is also clever. He thinks for a few seconds and then announces, correctly, the colour of his hat.

What colour hat is the blind man wearing? How did he know?

99. ABOVE OR BELOW

The first 25 letters of the alphabet are written out as shown below—with some letters above the line and some below. Where should Z go: above the line or below, and why?

A EF HI KLMN T VWXY

BCD G J OPQRS U

100. STRANGE SYMBOLS

When Alice first stepped through the looking glass, she saw this strange set of symbols on a sign:

"What does it mean?" she wondered. "It looks like a secret code or the alphabet of some foreign language." Alice studied the sign a little longer and then had a thought. "It's a sequence with a definite pattern." When you recognize the pattern you should have no difficulty in drawing the next figure in the sequence. What is the next symbol?

101. PRODUCT

What is the product of the following series?

$$(x-a)(x-b)(x-c)\ldots(x-z)$$

102. WHAT ARE THEY?

"How much does one cost?" asked the customer in a hardware store.

"Twenty pence," replied the clerk.

"And how much will twelve cost?"

"Forty pence."

"OK. I'll take nine hundred and twelve."

"Fine. That will be sixty pence."

What was the customer buying?

103. MENDING THE CHAIN

Alice has 4 pieces of gold chain, each consisting of 3 links. She wants to have the pieces joined together to make a necklace.

The jeweller tells her, "I charge £1 to break a link and £1 to melt it together again. To fit these pieces together, I'll have to break and rejoin four links. That will be £8."

Alice knows she has less than £7. "I don't have enough money," she says sadly and prepares to leave the shop.

Just then the jeweller says, "Wait, I've thought of another way." Sure enough, he has. How does he do it, and how much does he charge?

104. FAST FLY

A Ferrari is traveling at 30 miles per hour on a head-on collision course with a Maserati, which is being driven at a leisurely 20 miles per hour. When the two cars are exactly 50 miles apart, a very fast fly leaves the front fender of the Ferrari and travels towards the Maserati at 100 miles per hour. When it reaches the Maserati, it instantly reverses direction and flies back to the Ferrari and continues winging back and forth between the rapidly approaching cars. At the moment the two cars collide, what is the total distance the fly has covered?

105. HOW FAST?

The Baja Road Race is 1,000 miles long. At the half-way point, Speedy Gonzales calculates that he has been driving at an average speed of 50 miles per hour. How fast should he drive the second half of the race if he wants to attain an overall average of 100 miles per hour?

106. WHICH COFFEEPOT?

A camper is trying to decide which of two coffeepots (pictured below) to buy. He wants the one that will hold the most coffee.

Which one do you recommend? (Assume that the cross sections of the two coffeepots are exactly the same.)

107. COCKTAIL

Four toothpicks and a penny are arranged as shown above, to represent a cherry in an old-fashioned glass. Move 2 toothpicks and get the cherry outside of the glass. The glass may have any position at the end, but the cherry cannot be moved.

108. THE EXPLORER AND THE BEAR

You may have come across this well-known riddle.

An explorer walked 1 mile due south, turned and walked 1 mile due east, turned again and walked 1 mile due north. He found himself back where he started, and was then eaten by a bear. Question: What colour was the bear?

The answer is "White," because he must have started at the North Pole, so the bear that ate him must have been a polar bear.

However, the North Pole is not the only starting point that satisfies the conditions of the riddle. From what other point on the globe can you walk 1 mile south, 1 mile east, 1 mile north and find yourself at your original location?

109. BUTTONS AND BOXES

Imagine you have 3 boxes, one containing 2 red buttons, one containing 2 green buttons, and the third, 1 red button and 1 green button. The boxes are labelled according to their contents—RR, GG and RG. However, the labels have been switched so that each box is now incorrectly labelled. Without looking inside, you may take 1 button at a time out of any box. Using this process of sampling, what is the smallest number of buttons needed to determine the contents of all 3 boxes?

110. MANHATTAN AND YONKERS

Amy lives near Riverdale station. She has two boyfriends, Rob in Yonkers and Tony in Manhattan. To visit Rob, she takes a the northbound platform; to visit Tony she takes a train from the southbound platform. Since Amy likes both boys equally well, she always gets on the first train that comes along and lets chance determine whether she goes to Yonkers or Manhattan. Amy reaches the station at a random moment every Saturday afternoon. The northbound and southbound trains arrive at the station equally often—every 10 minutes. Yet, for some reason, she spends most of her time with Rob in Yonkers. In fact, on average, she goes there 9 times out of 10. Can you explain why the odds are so heavily in Rob's favour?

111. COUNTERFEIT COINS

In the figure below are 10 stacks of coins, each consisting of 10 silver dollars. One entire stack is counterfeit, but you do not know which one. You do know the weight of a genuine silver dollar, and you are also told that each counterfeit coin weighs 1 gram more or less than a genuine coin. You have a pointer scale which you use to weigh the coins.

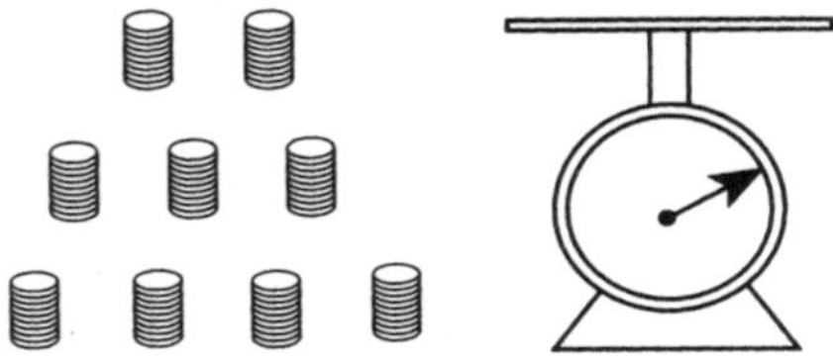

What is the smallest number of weighings needed to determine which of the stacks is counterfeit?

112. FAKE!

Here is another counterfeit coin puzzle.

One of 12 identical-looking coins is counterfeit. The weight of the counterfeit coin is different from that of the genuine coins. Using only a simple balance, how can the counterfeit coin be identified in just 3 weighings?

113. HOW LONG?

A bolt of cloth is coloured as follows: one-third and one-quarter of it are black, the other 8 metres are gray. How long is the bolt?

114. ARITHMETIC PROBLEM

In order to encourage his son to study arithmetic, a father agrees to pay his boy 8 pence for every problem correctly solved and to fine him 5 pence for each incorrect solution. At the end of 26 problems, neither owes anything to the other. How many problems did the boy solve correctly?

115. THE CLOAK

A butler is promised £100 and a cloak as his wages for a year. After 7 months he leaves this service, and receives the cloak and £20 as his due. How much is the cloak worth?

116. WATERLILIES

A particular waterlily reproduces by dividing into two every day. Thus on the first day we have 1, on the second day we have 2, on the third 4, on the fourth 8, and so on. If, starting with one waterlily, it takes 30 days to cover a certain area, how long will it take to cover the same area if we start with 2 waterlilies?

117. TWO STEAMERS

Two steamers simultaneously leave New York for Lisbon, where they spend 5 days before returning to New York. The first makes 30 knots going and 40 knots returning. The second makes 35 knots each way. Which steamer gets back first?

118. UNEQUAL SCALES

Discovering his scales are faulty, a grocer resolves to weigh all his customers' orders in two halves, putting the first half in the left-hand pan and weights in the right, then reversing the procedure. This, he believes, will be fair to both his customers and himself. Is he right?

119. THE LONG DIVISION

(This type of puzzle is called a cryptogram.)

I was sitting at my chessboard pondering a combination of moves. At my side were my son, aged 8, and my daughter, 4 years old. The boy was busy with his homework, which consisted of some exercises in long division, but he was rather handicapped by his mischievous sister, who kept covering up his figures with chessmen. As I looked up, only two digits remained visible (see below).

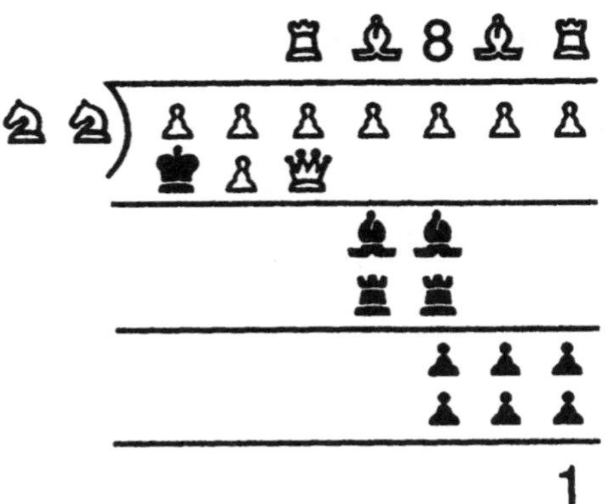

Can you calculate the missing digits without removing the chessmen?

120. TWO BOLTS

Below are two identical bolts held together with their threads in mesh. While holding bolt A stationary, you swing bolt B around it anticlockwise, as shown.

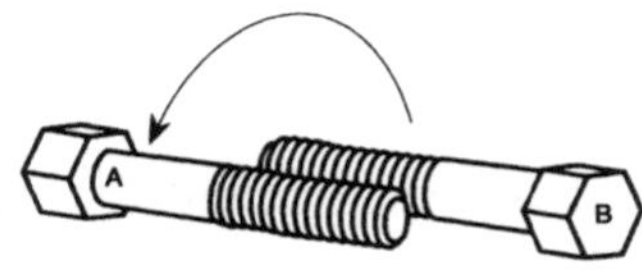

Will the bolt heads get nearer, move farther apart, or stay the same distance from each other? What will happen if you swing bolt B the opposite way—in a clockwise direction around A?

121. SURVIVING A DUEL

Lord Montcrief, Sir Henry Darlington and the Baron of Rockall decided to resolve a quarrel by fighting an unusual sort of pistol duel. They drew lots to determine who fired first, who second and who third. They then took their places at the corners of an equilateral triangle. It was agreed that they would fire single shots in turn and continue in the same order until two of them were dead. The man whose turn it was to fire could aim at either of the other two. It was known that Lord Montcrief always hit his target, that Sir Henry was 80 percent accurate and that the Baron was only 50 percent accurate.

Assuming that all three adopted the best strategy, and that no one was killed by a wild shot not intended for him, which one had the best chance of surviving?

122. FAIR SHARES

"Der Eine dielet, der Andere kieset."

This is an old German saying which prescribes how to divide a cake between two people and ensure that both of them are satisfied. The translation is: "One divides, the other chooses."

Can you devise a procedure so that *n* persons can divide a cake between them and each one is satisfied that he has obtained at least $^1/_n$ of the cake?

123. RACING DRIVER

A racing driver drove around a 6-mile track at 140 miles per hour for 3 miles, 168 miles per hour for 1.5 miles, and 210 miles per hour for 1.5 miles. What was his average speed for the entire 6 miles?

124. THE SIDE VIEW

Look at these two views of an object. What is the side view like? A perspective view?

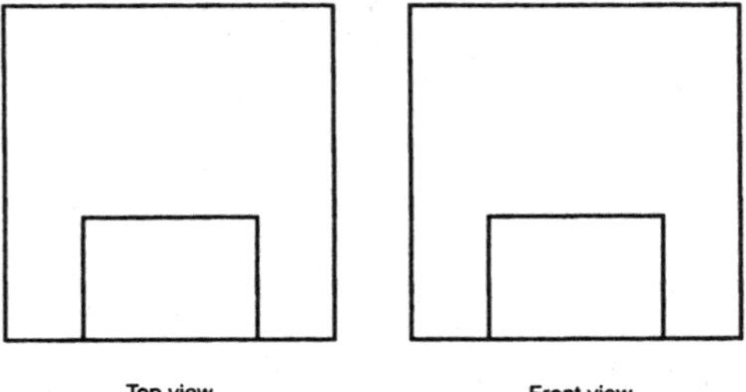

FALLACIES & PARADOXES

FALLACIES & PARADOXES

Man is an embodied paradox, a bundle of contradictions.

–Charles Caleb Colton (1780–1832)

The following conundrums offer a fascinating collection of mind-bending problems, and although the words "fallacies" and "paradoxes" are sometimes used interchangeably they are fundamentally different concepts.

Fallacy An argument involving logically invalid reasoning leading to a false conclusion. In most cases only one in a sequence of premises is flawed.

A simple example often used in various guises is to prove that $1 = 2$. This can only materialize if, through a number of arithmetical operations, we arrive at $1x = 2x$. This equation is indeed correct, provided that $x = 0$. I won't bore the reader with an actual exercise, as this elementary fallacy is not very interesting. There are others which will require a great deal of reasoning to find the flawed premise.

Paradox A situation which leads to contradictory conclusions that, more often than not, cannot be resolved (except perhaps on a philosophical plane).

The most famous, and by now classic, example is the liar paradox. Epimenides, who is from Crete, claims: "All Cretans are liars." No logical reasoning can determine whether the statement is true or false. In fact, it is both or neither.

Some examples are paradoxical on paper only, like Zeno's Paradox (described later), which, in real life, disappears. The reasoning process is one of explanation rather than solution. Many of these paradoxes are linked to such famous names as Galileo, Euclid and Aristotle, and have become part of intellectual history.

125. THE ODDS

Tom and Dick, compulsive gamblers, will bet on anything that offers odds, whereby the odds they propose to each other are rarely in line with the rules of probability.

One day Tom visited Dick and suggested a little bet. He put three playing cards face down on the table. "One of them," he explained to Dick, "is a Joker, the other two are aces. Draw a card without looking. One of the two cards remaining on the table must be an ace, which I turn over. Now the Joker is either on the table or is the one you have drawn. If the Joker is yours, I pay you £11; if it is the one on the table, you pay me £10."

Should Dick accept the bet?

126. THE DICE

Gambling with dice goes back to the sixteenth century, although in the early days of this particular game of chance the theory of probability was not yet developed. One player was at a loss to understand why, when three dice were thrown, 10 came up more frequently than 9, although the number of combinations are the same.

The total of 9 can be obtained by:

1 + 2 + 6, 1 + 3 + 5, 1 + 4 + 4, 2 + 2 + 5, 2 + 3 + 4, 3 + 3 + 3
= 6 combinations

A total of 10 is the result of:

$$1 + 3 + 6,\ 1 + 4 + 5,\ 2 + 2 + 6,\ 2 + 3 + 5,\ 2 + 4 + 4,\ 3 + 3 + 4$$
$$= 6 \text{ combinations}$$

The gambler approached Galileo (1564-1642), the famous Italian mathematician, who soon solved the mystery.

Can you do as well?

127. THE THREE-COIN FALLACY

You are tossing three coins. The probability that all three coins come down heads is clearly $^1/_2 \times {}^1/_2 \times {}^1/_2 = {}^1/_8$. The same applies, of course, to tails, i.e., $^1/_8$. Hence, the probability that all coins come down either heads or tails must be $^1/_4$.

So far, so good. But now consider this:

Of all three coins thrown up, at least two must show either heads or tails. The probability that the third also comes down the same as the other two must be $^1/_2$, because there are only two possibilities for the third coin — namely, heads or tails. Hence, we come to the surprising conclusion that the probability that all coins come down alike is $^1/_2$ and not $^1/_4$ as previously stated.

Can you solve the mystery?

128. ZENO'S PARADOX OR ACHILLES AND THE TORTOISE

This well-known classic is included because it exemplifies the very essence of a paradox. It was developed by Zeno the Stoic (320–250 B.C.), who was a native of Citium in Cyprus and studied under Crates the Cynic. Zeno's teachings embraced the dogmatic and paradoxical, rather than philosophical concepts.

Zeno described a hypothetical race between Achilles and a tortoise who would be given a head start of 1,000 metres. However, although Achilles could run ten times faster than the tortoise, he would never be able to overtake the animal. The argument ran as follows:

When Achilles had run the 1,000 metres, the tortoise would still be 100 metres ahead. When Achilles had gone the next 100 metres, the tortoise would still be 10 metres in front. This process would continue, with the tortoise one tenth of the distance ahead which Achilles had run.

This reasoning is clearly paradoxical. How would you counter Zeno's argument?

129. THE ROULETTE FALLACY

They say that there is no system which beats the house, mused Henry, but I can prove that, in fact, there is, and I have proved my theory more than a dozen times. It is actually quite simple. I only play the *chances simples* (even-money bets), either red/black or odd/even.

Let us say that I have $1,000 in cash on me and that I start by betting $20 on red. If I win, I then bet $10 the second time. But if I lose, I bet $30. I continue increasing or decreasing my bet by fifty percent as the case may be.

I have tried the system again and again using a pack of fifty-two bridge cards, and have even included a joker to represent the zero which is the house percentage, and I have always come out on top. Try it yourself, and if using fifty-two cards is too tedious, try it with six, eight or ten cards. You can even add a joker, whereby you should remember that zero loses only half the stake. (The French croupiers call it *en prison*.)

Why, then, does this ingenious system not give you an easy living?

130. THE MARBLE PARADOX

This famous paradox involving four marbles has caused much argument. Four marbles are placed in a box. One is white, one yellow, and two are blue. You draw two marbles, look at them, and put a blue marble on the table. You then ask the audience to calculate the chances that the other marble you have hidden in your hand is also blue. Most will see this puzzle as disappointingly simple, and argue thus:

There are three marbles left, one of each colour. Therefore, the probability that the marble in your hand is blue must be one in three.

Do you agree?

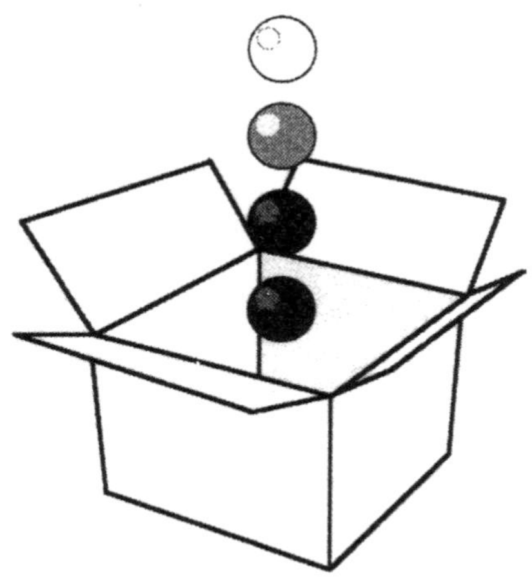

131. THE SERIES PARADOX

Study the fraction below, whereby the denominator is an infinite series. Hint: The answer has both a maximum and a minimum value. Can you find them?

$$\frac{1}{6 - 6 + 6 - 6 + 6 - 6 + 6 \ldots \infty}$$

132. THE SEVERED ARM

A well-dressed man, let's call him John, enters a bar in the Bowery in Manhattan in autumn 1945. After looking around, he sits down next to a down-and-out-looking man, obviously the worse for drink. John strikes up a conversation and orders another round of drinks.

After some small talk, John makes the following proposition to the stranger: "I am willing to give you $20,000 in cash, and pay to have you fitted with an artificial limb, if you agree to have your left forearm amputated."

After some hesitation, the stranger agrees and they proceed to a dingy office in the Bowery, where John introduces the stranger to a third man, who performs the surgery.

Following the surgery, John packs the severed limb in dry ice and sends the parcel to an address in Los Angeles. At the same time, he sends cables to a number of addresses on the West Coast. Several days later eight men meet in LA. The parcel is opened, its contents inspected. The men express satisfaction and disperse.

Find an explanation to fit these facts.

133. THE LIFT STOPPED

A woman leaves her flat, situated on the tenth floor of a high-rise building. She calls the lift and begins to descend. The lift comes to an abrupt stop between the fourth and third floors, and the light goes out. At that moment the woman's face turns ashen and she exclaims: "Oh God, my husband's dying."

Explain.

134. THE BARBER SHOP

After leaving work one evening, David looks in on a barber shop on his route home. The barber shop is a one-man business, and, on that evening, the proprietor is shaving a customer and has a long line of other customers waiting their turn.

"How long will you be?" David asks. The barber, after a little reflection, replies, "Hour. Hour and a half."

David thanks him and leaves.

A few days later, David checks out the barber shop again. This time the barber estimates he will be able to get to David in about 40 minutes. Once again, David thanks him and leaves.

The following day, the barber is just finishing with the last customer. "Give me 30 seconds," he tells David. David thanks the barber, but, instead of waiting, leaves the shop.

Explain.

135. THE CAR CRASH

Harry Jones was driving home in his car, with his son Robert in the passenger seat. The car was involved in a head-on collision with a lorry, killing Harry outright. Robert was seriously injured and taken to hospital by ambulance. In the hospital operating theatre, his would-be surgeon took one look at Robert and said, "I'm sorry, but I can't operate on this patient—he's my son." What is the explanation?

136. A GLASS OF WATER

A man enters a bar and asks for a glass of water.

The bartender draws a gun and shoots into the ceiling.

The man thanks him and walks out.

Is the bartender crazy? Is the man? Or is this just another day in Dodge City?

137. THE UNFAITHFUL WIFE

Charles, a bestselling author of romantic fiction, had suspected for some time that his wife Eva was being unfaithful, although he had no proof.

One afternoon, while Charles was working on his latest bodice-ripper, Eva mentioned that she intended to go to the cinema and would be out for a few hours. As Eva went to the door, Charles looked at her pensively, then resumed his work.

Three hours later, Eva returned, took her coat off and asked Charles whether he wanted some coffee. When she returned from the kitchen, Charles asked her to sit down as he wanted to talk to her.

"Eva," he said, "I want a divorce."

Why?

138. THE SUICIDE

The heiress to the Stanhope toothpaste fortune was found dead by her husband one morning, hanging from a chandelier in the master bathroom of their opulent townhouse. Her death had the police mystified. Suicide, the initial theory, was ruled out because there seemed no way she could have hanged herself. There was no furniture directly beneath or close to the body, nothing that looked like it had been kicked away; the toilet was fifteen feet away in a corner; the bath and Jacuzzi were both sunken into the floor. In short, the police found nothing that the deceased might have used to stand on.

Murder was a possibility—she had many enemies but there were no signs of forced entry, and she was a recluse who never had visitors. Besides, her husband—the only other resident—claimed that when he returned home after spending the night at his parents, he'd found the bathroom door locked from the inside and had had to break it down.

Detective-Sergeant Plod had his suspicions about the husband, but nothing could be proved. The inquest handed down an open verdict, which enabled the husband to collect millions on his wife's life insurance.

Plod became obsessed with the case until his dying day, convinced that the husband must either have been involved, in some way, in the heiress's death, or at least have concealed evidence of her suicide before calling the police, thereby defrauding the insurance company. Was Plod right?

139. THE DEADLY SCOTCH

Mr. El and Mr. Lay went into a bar and each ordered a scotch on the rocks. Unknown to them, they both got drinks laced with poison. Mr. El downed his in one gulp and proceeded to chat for an hour while Mr. Lay drank his slowly. Later, Mr. Lay died, but Mr. El didn't. Why?

140. THE TWO ACCOUNTANTS

Smith and Jones are partners in a small firm of accountants managing the investments of rock music stars. Jones is eight years Smith's senior, but is actually the junior partner, having joined the firm after Smith.

One morning, just before Christmas, Smith's secretary bursts into the conference room, where Smith and Jones are in a meeting, in search of her boss. "Your son just called," the secretary says. "Apparently, there's been a change of plan and you're going to your in-laws for the holiday."

On hearing this, Jones paled, got hold of a paperweight and threw it at his partner. Why?

141. THE ANTIQUE CANDELABRUM

The scene is a famous antique dealer's in London. A Rolls-Royce pulls up and a liveried chauffeur opens the door to a distinguished-looking elderly man, who enters the shop.

He points at a seventeenth-century candelabrum in the window. He examines it closely and then engages in an animated dialogue with the dealer. Eventually, he writes a check for £5,000 and departs with the candelabrum.

Shortly thereafter the dealer makes a number of telephone calls before closing his shop. Two days later, he receives a call which clearly pleases him.

In the meantime, the distinguished-looking man has carefully wrapped the candelabrum he bought. A younger man, Robert, arrives at his suite at the Ritz and takes the wrapped candelabrum by taxi to the same antique dealer from whom the older man bought it. The dealer pays him £9,000 in cash for the candelabrum.

What happened?

142. THE LIFT JOCKEY

After reading about the death of jogging guru Jim Fixx, Bill eschewed all forms of exercise, considering it harmful to his health. He set up the International League of Couch-Potatoes and campaigned tirelessly on behalf of a sedentary lifestyle. His message soon struck a chord with a public tired of being harangued into doing exercise, to the point where business within the fitness industry began to suffer. Several of the country's largest health club chains and sports equipment manufacturers joined forces to combat the Couch-Potato movement; they spent lavishly on advertising, and put a private detective on Bill's tail in the hope of unearthing something to discredit him.

After six weeks of round-the-clock surveillance, the detective triumphantly submitted his report. While Bill seemed to follow his credo to the letter in public, the detective had noticed that when Bill took the lift up to his flat on the twenty-third floor of his building alone, he had a habit of getting out on the fifteenth floor and walking—one could almost call it jogging—up the last eight floors. He never did this, the report noted, if there were other people in the lift. The detective had even managed to sneak a few photographs!

The story and the photos were leaked to the press, and Bill's reputation within Couch-Potato circles was ruined. However, he sued for libel and won. How come?

143. THE CROSSROADS

George Genti was very proud of his new turbo coupe Rover as he drove north from Tunbridge towards Orpington. He was travelling at 50 miles per hour, well within the speed limit, and as he had just landed a profitable contract, he hadn't a care in the world. As he was about to pass the Hadlow crossing, a black Nissan, traveling at high speed, collided with his Rover, severely damaging his car.

George, knowing he had right of way, was furious. He was on the point of blasting the driver of the Nissan with an effusion of four-letter words, when a gorgeous creature stepped out of the Nissan and, with the sweetest of smiles, accepted full responsibility and apologized profusely.

They moved their cars off the road, so as not to impede traffic and continued to chat. George was utterly captivated by the charm of this beautiful woman.

After exchanging first names she suggested that they celebrate their newfound friendship with a drop of the best. She produced a bottle of Grand Marnier and two glasses which she filled to the brim and toasted: "To us—bottoms up." George was happy to oblige, but was perplexed to see that she poured her own drink onto the ground.

Why did she behave so offensively?

VISUAL-SPATIAL TEST

VISUAL-SPATIAL TEST

Not puzzles in the traditional sense, the visual-spatial items on the following pages do make demands on your cognitive ability. Taken together, as a test, they are subject to timing and you are expected to solve the 34 items in 30 minutes.

You will find similar examples in most IQ test batteries, consequently the results here will be a reasonable indication as to your performance in standardized and validated tests. It would be presumptuous to translate the number of correct answers (even strictly within the time allowed) into an IQ score. However, after you check your answers against the solutions, the following evaluation can be a useful guide.

Answers correct:
Above 30 – Excellent
27 – 29 – Very Good
24 – 26 – Good
21 – 23 – Fair
18 – 20 – Average

Now, if you are up for a test, prepare yourself and turn the page to start. Remember, you have 30 minutes to complete it, just under a minute for each test item.

144. Identify the two shapes which, by turning them around but not turning over, could cover each other.

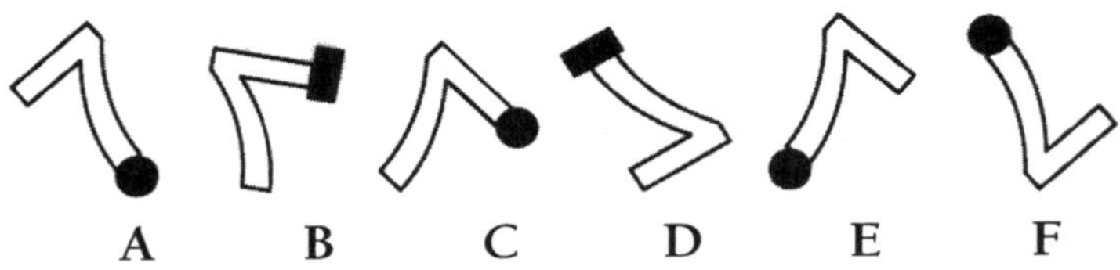

145. Identify the two shapes which, without turning them over, cannot cover the other four shapes.

VISUAL-SPATIAL TEST

In the following four puzzles, identify the odd man out.

146.

A B C D E

147.

A B C D E

148.

A B C D E

149.

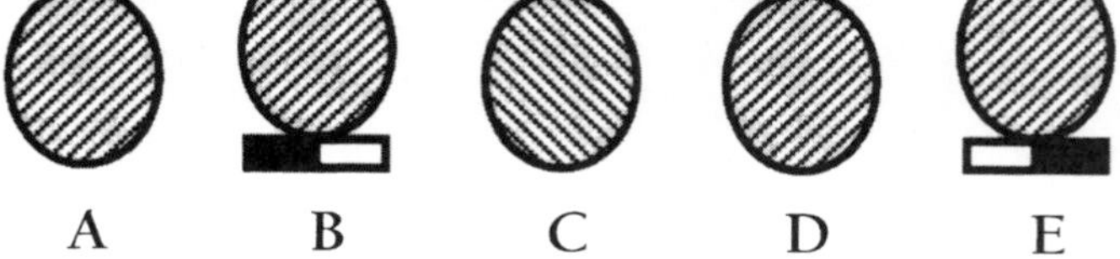

A B C D E

150. Identify the odd man out.

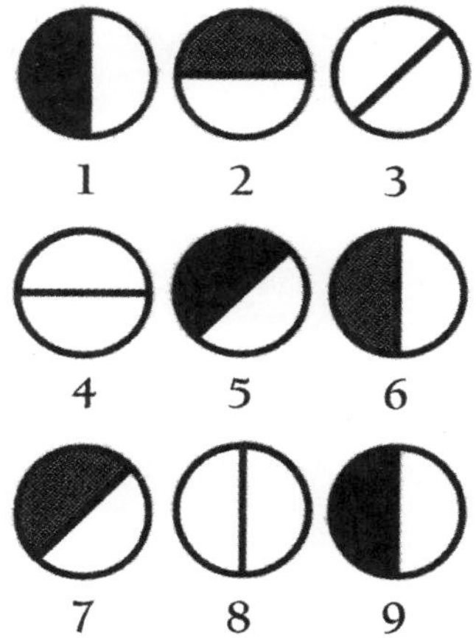

151. Find the odd man out.

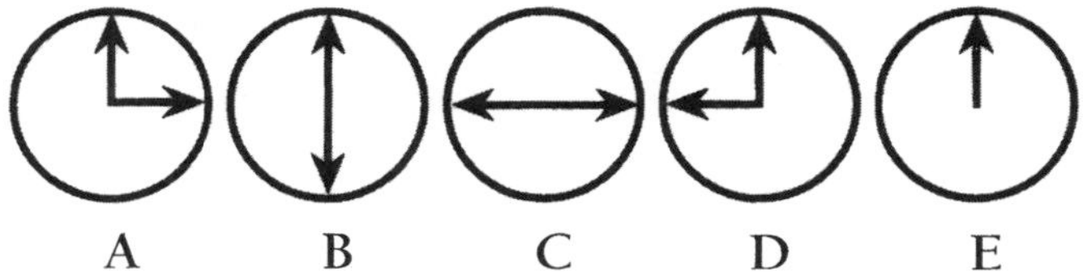

152. Find the odd man out.

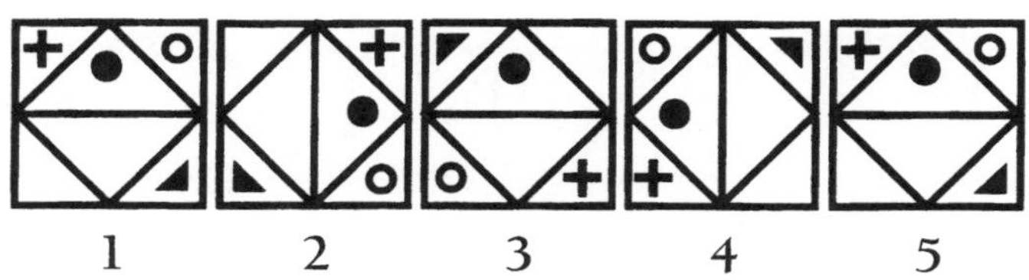

153. Which of the lettered figures is the odd man out?

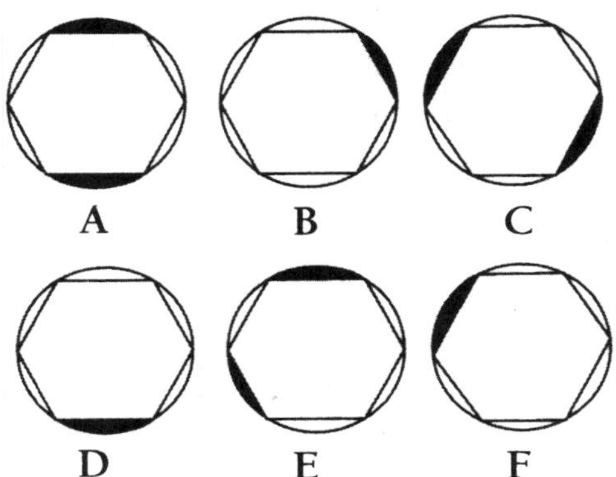

154. Which of the figures does not fit in with the others?

155. Which figure differs from all the others in a material aspect?

156. Find the three which are different from the other four.

157. Select the correct figure from the lettered ones to complete the set.

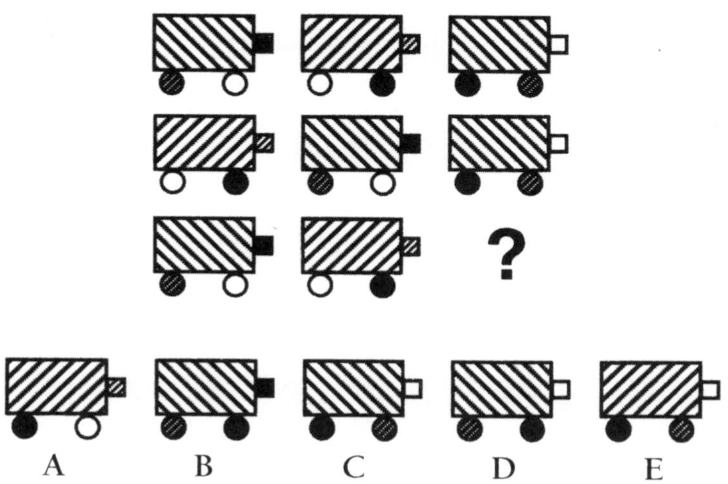

158. Which of the numbered figures completes the series?

?

1 2 3 4 5

159. Select the correct figure from the six lettered ones.

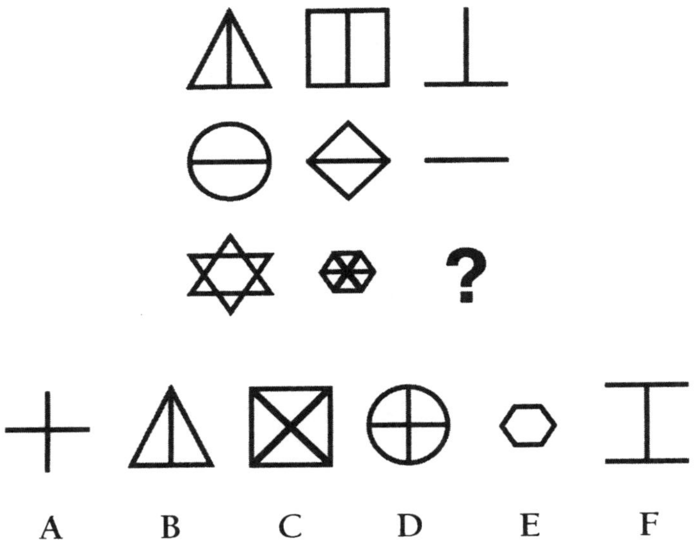

160. Identify the correct figure from the six lettered ones.

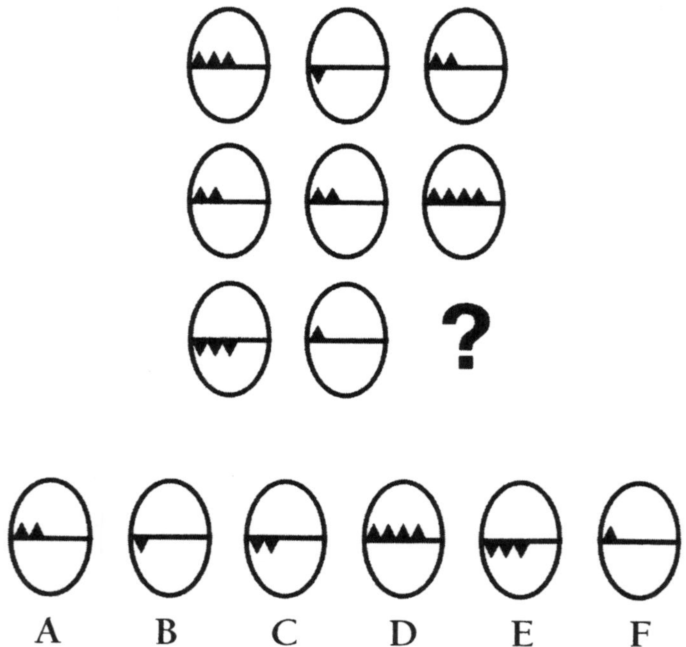

161.

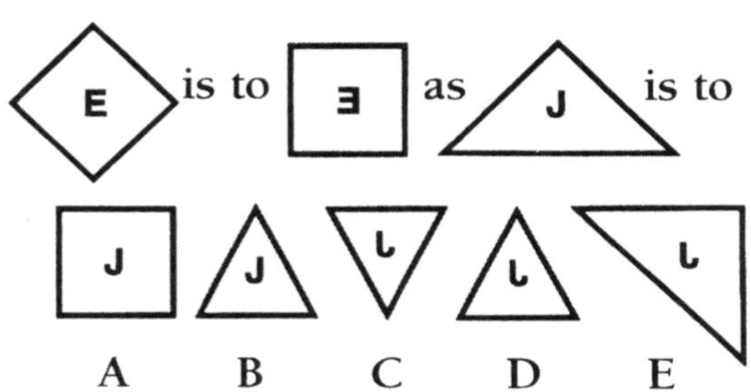

162.

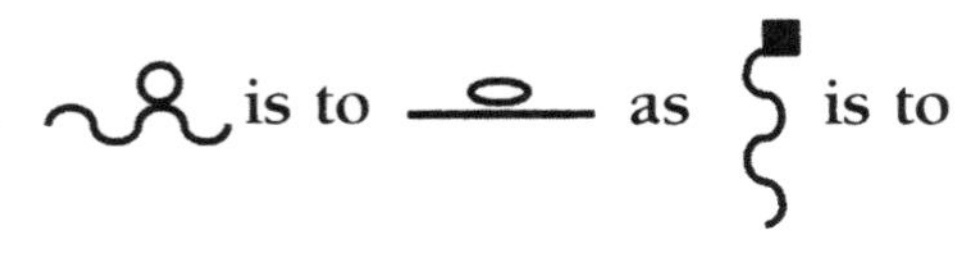

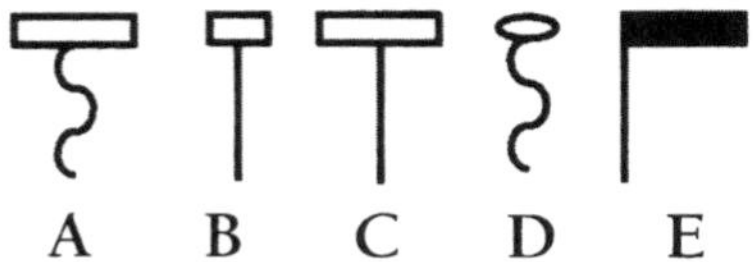

163. **LMNO** is to **OMNL** as **WXYZ** is to

XYZW	**ZYXW**	**WXYZ**	**ZXYW**	**YZWX**
A	B	C	D	E

164.

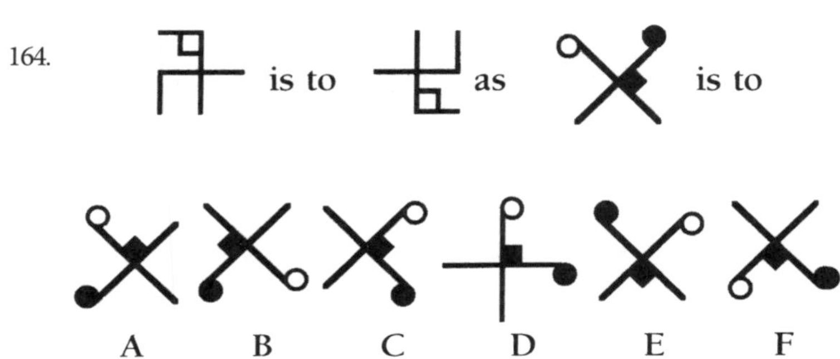

165.

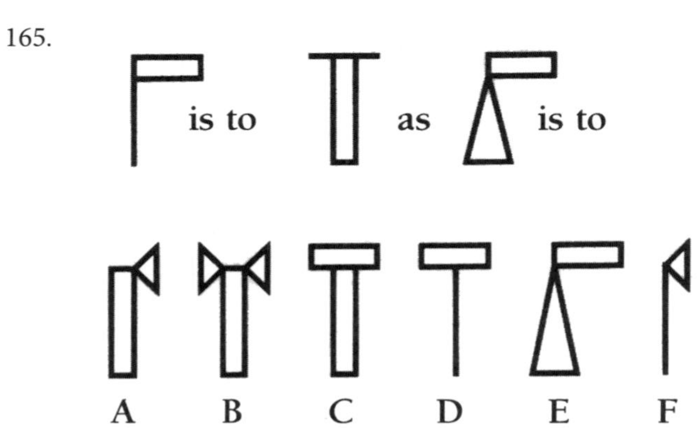

166. Which of the lettered figures will complete the sequence?

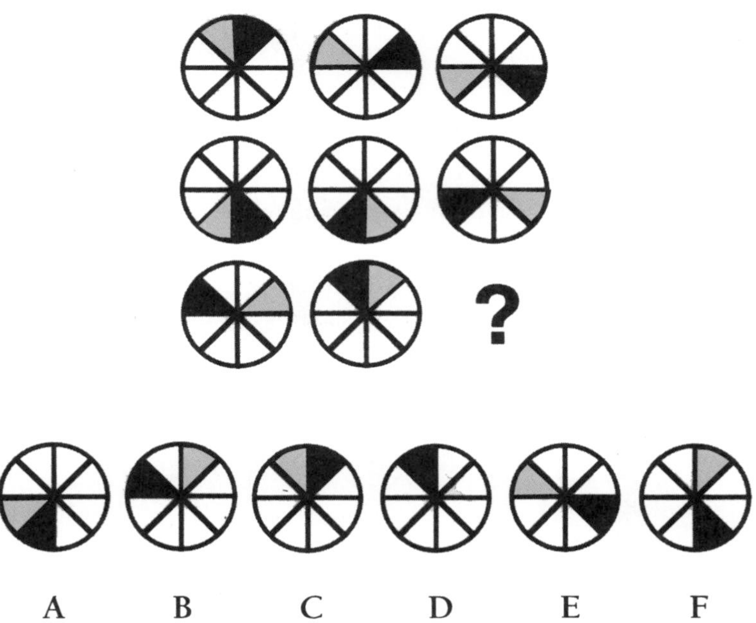

For questions 167 and 168 following, identify the two shapes on the right which can be rotated into the shape set off on the left side without turning over.

167.

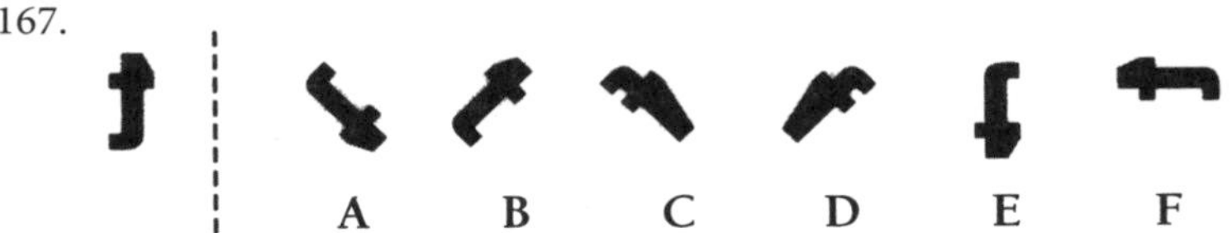

168.

169. Select the correct figure from the four numbered ones.

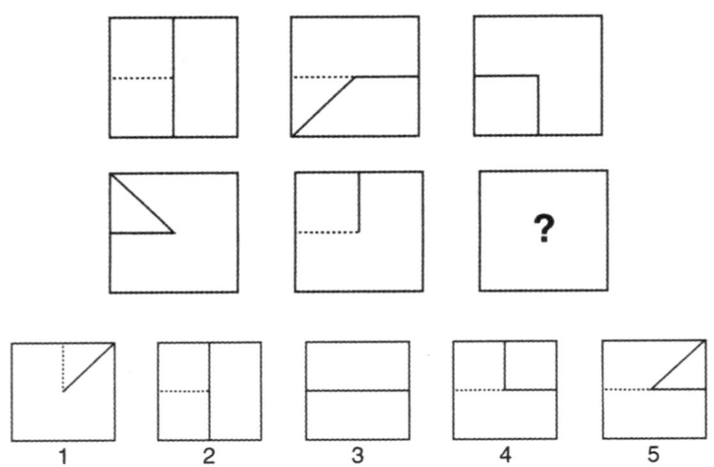

170. Find the two odd men out.

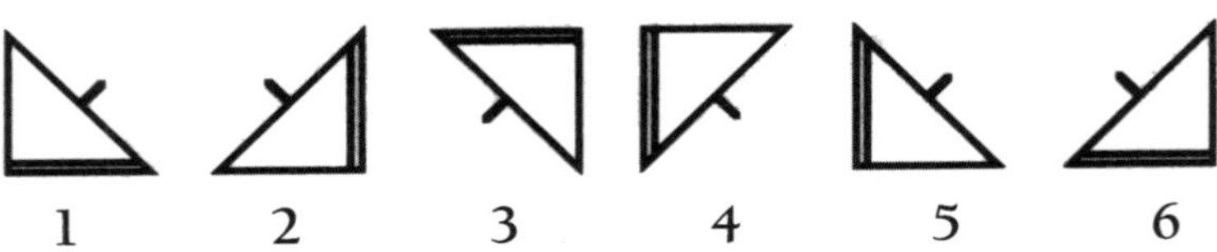

171. Identify the two groups which can be rotated into each other.

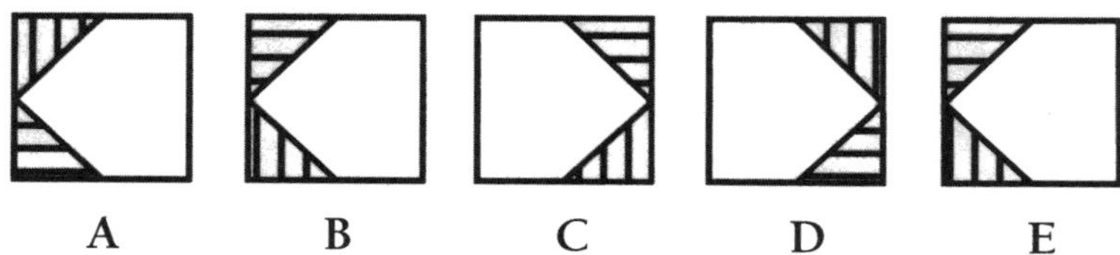

172. Identify the two odd men out.

173. Which of the lettered figures comes next?

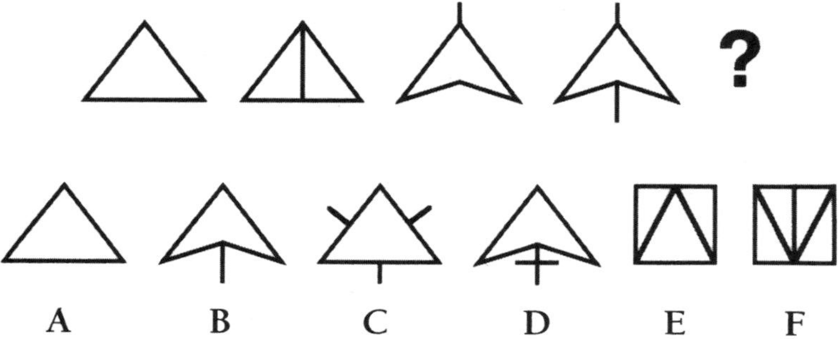

174. Which of the numbered shapes fits into the empty space?

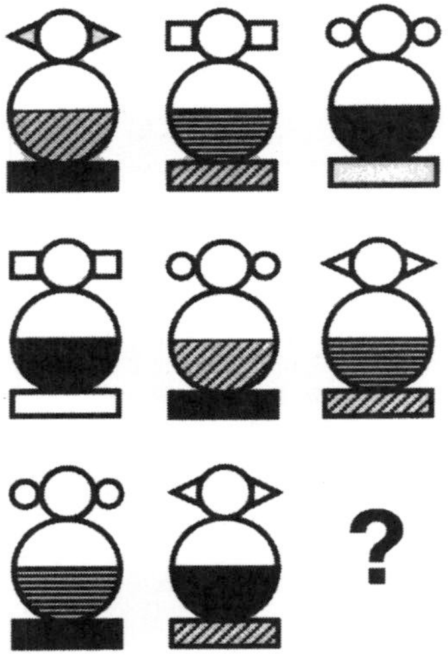

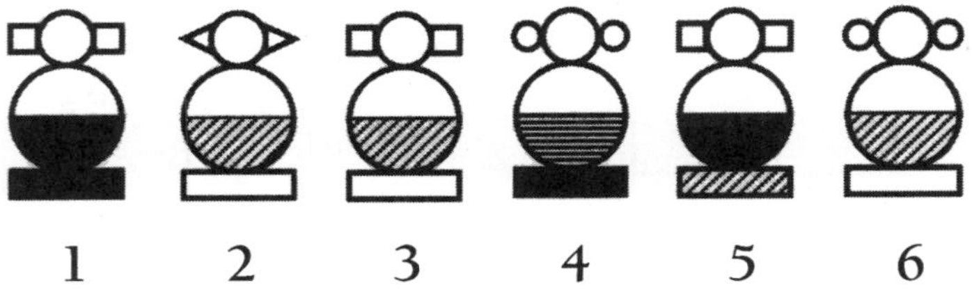

?

1 2 3 4 5 6

175. Which lettered shape will continue the series?

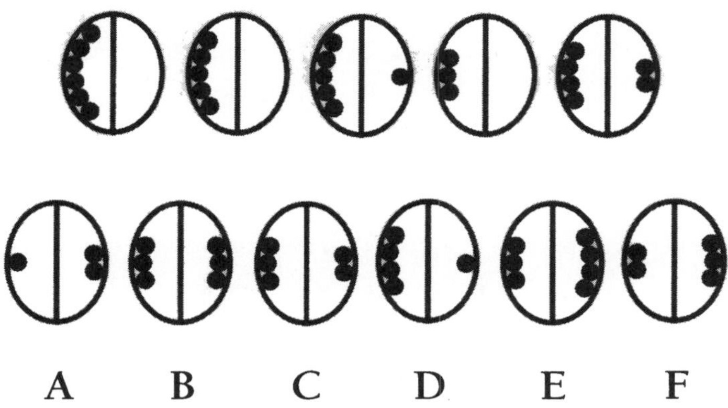

176. Which figure comes next in the series?

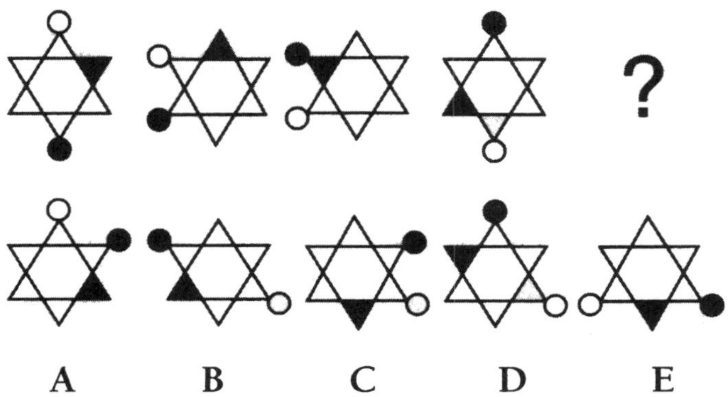

177. Which two letters do not belong?

L A V X M N C I

1 2 3 4 5 6 7 8

The test is completed. Compare your answers with the test solutions on pages XX–XX, and see page 82 for your evaluation.

SOLUTIONS

SOLUTIONS

1. LIARS AND TRUTH-TELLERS I

The question would be: "Is your friend a truth-teller?" Suppose Fred is the liar (L) and Harry the truth-teller (T) and you ask Fred. His answer would have to be "No." If you ask Harry (T) his answer would also be "No."

2. LIARS AND TRUTH-TELLERS II

The question to be asked of one of them is: "If I were to ask your friend whether he is a liar, what would be his answer?" Suppose you ask Fred (L), his answer would be "Yes." If, however, the question were directed to Harry (T), he would truthfully answer that Fred would deny being the liar. Consequently, "Yes" would identify the liar and "No" the truth-teller.

3. ANOTHER LIARS AND TRUTH-TELLERS

All members of the tribe would profess to be truth-tellers, no matter what in fact they were. Therefore, Chang must have been lying and Chung was telling the truth when he called him a liar. The pedigree of Ching remains a mystery, never to be resolved.

4. SIBLINGS

1. If Steve has one brother, then he must have two sisters —which does not work out. Let's try two brothers, in which case he must have four sisters. Each sister then has three brothers and three sisters as stated.
2. If Fred has one brother he must have three sisters, in which case each sister has as many brothers as sisters, namely two.

The method used above to arrive at these solutions is called "trial and error." A more systematic approach is available using the language of equations. Most readers will have no problem, but for those who are unfamiliar with this tool, or to whom equations are no more than a distant memory from school days, these two puzzles are an easy introduction to the simplicity and beauty of this alternative language. In Steve's family, let x be the number of boys and y the number of girls. Then Steve has $(x - 1)$ brothers and y sisters. Twice the number of sisters as brothers can be expressed as:

$$y = 2\,(x - 1)$$

But Joanna has (y – 1) sisters, who are equal to the number of brothers, i.e.,

$$(y - 1) = x \qquad \text{or} \qquad y = (x + 1)$$

Reduce the two equations above and you have:

$$x + 1 = 2x - 2$$

Therefore:

$$x = 3 \text{ and } y = 4$$

Now try to solve Fred's problem by the same method.

5. THE BRIDGE PARTY

The four played chamber music during dinner.

6. GOLDEN WEDDING

The sex of every member of the family has been identified except for the "cousin," who could be male or female.

7. THE ENCYCLOPEDIA

A little logic will avoid a laborious trial-and-error exercise.

1. The total number of coins must be divisible by four, since there cannot be a fraction of a coin in Henry's pocket.
2. The average must be less than 20, to meet the condition that Henry has three less than the average. In other words, the total in all four pockets will be less than 80.
3. Try the next lower total divisible by 4, which is 76. The average is 19, and Henry has 16 coins.

Using equation language, the same solution will be obtained as follows:

Let x be the number of coins in Henry's pocket. Then the average is $x + 3$ but it is also:

$$60 + x / 4$$

Thus:

$$x + 3 = 60 + x / 4$$

This can be reduced to:

$$4x + 12 = 60 + x, \text{ or } 3x = 48$$

Therefore $x = 16$

8. SECOND TIME AROUND

The answer is six. We immediately realize that the number of children common to Ellen and Richard must be even. If we try two plus eight we come to only twelve. Therefore, the answer is that each parent brought four children into the marriage, giving birth to another six thereafter.

In equation language:

Let x be the number of children common to both. As each parent was related by blood to ten children, they must have brought the same number into the marriage. Let this number be y.

Then:

1. $y + x = 10$

   and

2. $2y + x = 14$

Subtract formula 1 above from formula 2.

$y = 4$

$x = 10$

9. CLUB 54

Yes. Carla is eighteen years old. John worked it out in his head. If x is her present age, then in three years' time she will be $x + 3$, which, according to her, is $^3/_2$ times her age four years ago $(x - 4)$, or:

$$x + 3 = 3/2\ (x - 4)$$

This reduces to:

$$2x + 6 = 3x - 12, \text{ or } x = 18$$

10. A BOTTLE OF WINE

It's $^3/_4$ kg. Remove a bottle of wine from the left pan, and the only bottle from the right pan. The scale will still balance, making the weight of one bottle equal to half of $1^1/_2$ kg. The number of carats in the bars is irrelevant.

11. PENCIL, PAPER AND LOGIC

It will help to convert everything into thirds. Thus, the question is:

If $^{20}/_3$ were $^{24}/_3$ how much would $^{30}/_3$ be?

Clearly 20% more, or $^{36}/_3$, i.e. 12 or, in equation form:

$$\frac{20}{3} : \frac{24}{3} = \frac{30}{3} : \frac{3x}{3}$$

This reduces to $60x = 720$ or $x = 12$

12. JOE'S HIDEAWAY

On the assumption that the six meals do not have to be taken at one sitting, Fred would be better off to take two quests out twice as he would be entitled to one free meal on another occasion.

13. THE MONTE CARLO RALLY

The answer is 800 kilometres. Four tyres cover a total of 4,800 kilometres. However, this distance was spread over six tyres, resulting in 800 kilometres' wear each.

14. NEXT LETTER

M for March. The letters denote the months in reverse order.

15. THE TEST

Dick argued: If mine were white, Tom would see a white and a red disc and would realize that his own would have to be red because otherwise Harry would realize at once that his was red, seeing two white discs. As Tom did not step forward, Dick concluded that his disc must be red.

16. THE GAMBLERS

The beggar could have had no money, but certainly less than £1.

17. THE BARGAIN

They were £13 each. The selling price of the second watch was only £14 after the proceeds from the first watch, to realize a profit of £1. Consequently, the cost had to have been £13.

18. TRYING TO ESCAPE

George should have stood on Alfie's shoulders as his arms, being much longer, would have reached the railing.

19. THE LAWN

It would take two hours. It is really quite simple if you know how to approach it.

In one hour:

Adam would mow one twelfth of the lawn,

Danny one sixth,

and Fred one quarter of it.

In other words, fractionally speaking:

$^1/_{12} + ^1/_6 + ^1/_4$ of the lawn.

This simplifies to:

$^1/_{12} + ^2/_{12} + ^3/_{12} = ^6/_{12}$ or half in one hour.

20. SECOND AND THIRD

It is the third hand of a watch after the hour and minute hand, and it is called the second hand.

21. GUESSING THE ODDS

Simple: 1 in 52. It is easy to see if you assume that George turns his card over first. Your stack has 52 cards, and one of them will match George's card.

22. THE LONG DIVISION

It's 10. Start at the end and work towards the beginning. Nine-tenths of 100 is 90. Eight-ninths of 90 is 80. Seven-eighths of 80 if 70. And so on until you come to one-half of 20.

23. A STRANGE PRICING POLICY

The store charged £1 per letter for each item.

24. THE SURVEY

Only 10%. If you consider only those females having blue eyes, the minimum overlap would be 30%. These 30% would have a minimum overlap with fair-haired females of 10%.

The answer is immediately available by adding together all the percentages, i.e. 210, and deducting the product of one less than the three features (female, blue eyes, fair hair), i.e. 2 and 100. The product being 200, deducted from 210, gives the solution: 10%.

25. HEART AND ARROW

As trees grow at their tops, the love sign remained at the height Egon had carved it. Gloria was only ten when she could carve her initials, so Egon had to renege.

26. DIVIDE AND MULTIPLY

The answer is 60. If you don't agree, think again.

27. CLIMBING THE MATTERHORN

Harry carried the equipment for 2 kilometres more than Fred.

Let x be the distance from base camp to the peak. Then:

Fred carried for 4 kilometres + $(x - 5)$ km = $x - 1$ km

Harry carried for 5 kilometres + $(x - 4)$ km = $x + 1$ km

The interesting aspect of this puzzle is that the difference is always 2 kilometres, irrespective of the distance x.

28. UNUSUAL FRACTIONS

A. $\frac{1}{\infty}$ 0. The larger the denominator, the smaller the fraction. Approaching infinity, the fraction tends towards zero.

B. $\frac{1}{0}$ ∞. The smaller the denominator, the larger the fraction.

C. $\frac{\infty}{0}$ The same principle as B.

D. $\frac{\infty}{\infty}$ Any number divided by itself is 1.E. $\frac{0}{\infty}$ Zero divided by any number is zero.

F. $\frac{0}{0}$ The same principle as E.

29. A HEAVY SMOKER

On the second, third, fourth and fifth days he increased the original number of cigarettes by 6, 12, 18 and 24 respectively, a total of 60. The balance of 60 to account for the total consumption of 120 is again 60 spread over five days. He started, therefore, with 12 cigarettes.

30. RELATION

My mother.

31. THE WATER-SKIER

Downstream, he covers 1 kilometre in 2 minutes. Upstream, he only does $^1/_2$ a kilometre in the same time. Therefore, the current accelerates/decelerates by half the difference, i.e. $^1/_4$ kilometre in 2 minutes, or $7^1/_2$ kilometres per hour.

In still water, he could cover 3 kilometres in 8 minutes.

32. THE HUNGRY HUNTER

It would be wrong to share £3 and £5 respectively. This would be payment for the number of loaves the shepherds had originally. They should be paid for the loaves they gave to the hunter.

Each of the three ended up with $2^2/_3$ loaves. In other words, the first shepherd parted with $^1/_3$ of a loaf, and the other with $2^1/_3$ or $^7/_3$ loaves. Payment should, therefore, be £1 and £7 respectively.

33. THE LONELY FLIGHT

If the pilot flies along a meridian due north and then turns around, he will land 20 miles short of takeoff. If he flies over the North Pole and continues due south, which still means changing direction, he will land 820 miles from takeoff.

34. POOL RESOURCES

Jim has £5 and Andrew £7. There are two clues to the solution. The difference must be £2 to balance, and the original holdings must be odd numbers; otherwise, Andrew, having received £1, can never have twice Jim's amount.

Using an equation, let Jim's amount be x and Andrew's, y.

Then:

$$2(x - 1) = (y + 1)$$

and

$$(y - 1) = (x + 1)$$

or

$$y = x + 2$$

Therefore:

$$2(x - 1) = x + 3$$

$$2x - 2 = x + 3$$

$$x = 5$$

$$y = 7$$

35. ADD AND MULTIPLY

It is 3.

Let the number be x; then

$$x + \frac{3}{2} = \frac{3}{2} : x$$

or

$$2x + 3 = 3x$$

Therefore

$$x = 3$$

36. CATCHING THE TRAIN

John gets to the station first, while Fred is likely to miss the train. Let the actual time be 11:30 a.m.; then John's watch will show 11:35 while he thinks it is 11:45. Fred's watch will show 11:20 while he thinks it is 11:15.

37. TELL THE TIME

The meeting was at noon. As there are twelve hours between 3 a.m. and 3 p.m., the halfway mark would have been 9 a.m., which was stated to be three hours before the meeting time.

38. THE NEXT NUMBER

It's 17. Seventeen (9 letters), nineteen (8 letters), fifteen (7 letters), eleven (6 letters), etc.

39. FIND THE WORD

Sight. (All the words in the first line can be prefixed with "over," as can sight.)

40. THE SWISS SMUGGLERS

Customs received 24 cartons and £48 net (after paying Margaret £96). Of this, Titus was responsible for 60 percent, i.e. 14.4 cartons and £28.80. However, he paid £115.20 more, which must therefore compensate for 2.4 cartons (as he only surrendered 12). This works out at a cost of £48 per carton and a duty of £24.

The alternative approach is to use an equation.

Let x be the duty and y the cost per carton. Then:

$$30x = 12y + 144$$

and $$20x = 12y - 96$$

Deduct the lower equation from the one above and:

$$10x = 240$$

and $$x = 24$$

41. THE THREE DIGITS

The solution is 500. (Add the left and right numbers.)

42. ANALOGY

The analogy can be written thus:

$$5x : -8 = -10 : x$$

or $$5x = 80$$

$$x = 16$$

43. EARLY BURIAL

He was killed in December 1958 BC, and was buried a few days later in January 1957 BC.

44. THE AUCTION

It was a set of 12; $^2/_3$ or $^8/_{12}$ of which were scratched, $^1/_2$ or $^6/_{12}$ were chipped.

Of the glasses, $^1/_4$ or $^3/_{12}$ that were scratched and chipped were included in the $^{14}/_{12}$ and must, therefore, be deducted, resulting in $^{11}/_{12}$ damaged glasses. The one intact glass is, therefore, $^{11}/_{12}$ of the total.

The same result can be obtained by using an equation. Let x be the number of glasses in the set.

Then:

$$\frac{2x}{3} + \frac{1x}{2} - \frac{1x}{4} + 1 = x$$

Simplify to:

$$\frac{8x}{12} + \frac{6x}{12} - \frac{3x}{12} + \frac{12}{12} = \frac{12x}{12}$$

Therefore:

$$11x + 12 = 12x$$

and $x = 12$

45. THE GOLD COIN

It can't be box C because then both statements would be false. Therefore, the coin is in either box A or box B. If so, the first statements on both boxes agree and are therefore both either true or false. If they are fake then the second statements must both be true, which is impossible since they contradict each other. Therefore, the first statements on boxes A and B must both be correct, proving that the coin must be in box B.

46. STRANGE SYMBOLS

The next two symbols are:

The sequence consists of the first eight letters of the alphabet and their mirror images.

47. THE PIGGY BANK

This puzzle is more interesting and less complicated than it appears at first glance. Reasoning will provide a ready answer. James in fact returned all the coins he had picked up except four times the number of coins Henry had given him. In other words, he is left with 24 coins.

As an equation, let x be the number of coins picked up by Henry, and y the number of coins left to Henry.

Then:

$$y = 3x + 6 - 3\ (x - 6)$$
$$= 3x + 6 - 3x + 18$$

x conveniently cancels out, and

$$y = 24$$

The answer is therefore independent of the number of coins first picked up by Henry.

48. NEW YEAR'S EVE

The year was 1961.

49. THE CHANNEL TUNNEL

They are 260 kilometres apart, the combined distance the trains will travel in 40 minutes.

50. THE DELIVERY

At 60 miles per hour, the lorry covers a mile in one minute; at 30 miles per hour, it covers a mile in 2 minutes, or one minute slower per mile. The difference between the two arrival times is 120 minutes, accounted for by a speed difference of one minute per mile.

Consequently:

1: The customer's head office is 120 miles from Samson's warehouse.

2: It would be a mistake to think that the required speed to arrive at noon should be 45 miles per hour. At 60 miles per hour, the distance would be covered in 2 hours. The trip is to take an hour longer, or 120 miles divided by 3, or 40 miles per hour.

51. THE CROWDED TRAIN

The answer is two-thirds.

Let x be the duration of the journey. Joe first stood:

$$\frac{x}{2}$$

Of the remaining half, he stood one-third, or

$$\frac{x}{6}$$

$$\frac{x}{2} + \frac{x}{6} = \frac{4x}{6}$$

that is, two thirds of the journey.

52. THE RACE

Fred would arrive back at the first pole more than a minute before

Ernest reaches the tenth pole. The illustration makes it dear.

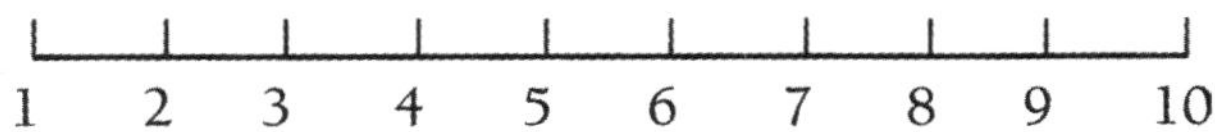

Fred, who has to run 8 kilometres, can do it in 48 minutes, while Ernest will do the 9 kilometres in just over 49 minutes.

53. RELATIONSHIP

It could be one of your brothers — or you yourself.

54. THE FRACTION

Quicker than trial and error is a simple equation.

Let x be the nominator, and y the denominator of the fraction we are trying to find.

Then:

$$\frac{4 \times x}{y} = \frac{x + y}{2y}$$

Simplify to:

$$8x = x + y$$

or

$$y = 7x$$

Therefore, the required fraction is

$$\frac{x}{7x} \text{ or } \frac{1}{7}$$

Proof (add 7 to top and bottom):

$$\frac{1}{7} + \frac{7}{7} = \frac{4}{7}$$

55. CHRISTMAS SHOPPING

1. Let us call the presents A, B and C, belonging to Margaret (M), Joan J) and Sheila (S) respectively There are six possibilities for distributing them among the ladies:

	1	2	3	4	5	6
M	A	A	B	B	C	C
J	B	C	A	C	A	B
S	C	B	C	A	B	A

It is clear from the above that only in cases 4 and 5 does no one get the right present, leaving four cases, i.e. two-thirds, in which at least one present goes to the right owner. 2. The probability is zero. If only one lady gets the wrong present, the other two must have the correct present, and therefore all presents go to the rightful owners.

56. DECK OF CARDS

If L1 had R red cards, then it had 3R black cards. Therefore, L2 had 26 – R red cards, and 36 - 3R black cards. Now you add 4 red cards to L2, which brings the number of red cards to 3 times the number of black cards. Therefore:

30 – R = 3 (26 – 3R)

R = 6 The deck was originally divided as follows:

L1: 6R / 18B

L2: 20R / 8B

57. THREE CARDS

This problem sounds far more complicated than it is. The deck of cards is a red herring. The question reduces to this: Take 3 cards, say 2, 3 and 4 of clubs, facedown. What is the probability of turning them over in the order 2, 3, 4? There are 6 possible ways of arranging 3 cards. Therefore, the probability is one-sixth.

58. YOUR VERY OWN

Your name.

59. THE CONFERENCE

There are two ways to solve this problem.

1. Graphically.
2. The different characteristics add up to 300, to be distributed among 100 people.
   You can apportion three features to each. Therefore, no person needs to have all four.

60. A FAMILY PUZZLE

There are four generations at tea.

Elsa is Jenny's mother.

Tom is Jenny's son.

Harry is Tom's son.

61. GUESS THE NUMBER

By reasoning: If $^5/_9$ is $^2/_3$ of the fraction, then $^5/_{18}$ is $^1/_3$, and $^{15}/_{18}$ or $^5/_6$ is the fraction.

Using an equation:

$$\frac{2x}{3} = \frac{5}{9}$$

or

$$\frac{6x}{9} = \frac{5}{9}$$

and

$$x = \frac{5}{6}$$

62. THE STABLE

Sam had three horses. Three-quarters of a horse must be the missing quarter of the number of horses.

Or, let x be the number of horses.

Then:

$$\frac{3x}{4} + \frac{3}{4} = x$$

Simplify:

$$3x + 3 = 4x$$

or $\quad x = 3$

63. THE PUNCTURE

Brian rides his bicycle half as far as the car goes, but it takes him three times as long. Therefore, the Ford Fiesta's speed is six times the speed of the bike.

64. THE DOLE

Let x and y respectively be the number of men and women in the town.

One third of men drew 45 each = $\frac{45x}{3}$

One half of women drew 30 each = $\frac{30y}{2}$

They were paid a total of 15,000 pounds; therefore:
$\frac{45x}{3} + \frac{30y}{2} = 15{,}000$
Simplified:
$15\,(x + y) = 15{,}000$
or $(x + y)$, which represents the population = 1,000

If you want to know more, a little trial-and-error exercise will tell you that there are 600 men and 400 women.

65. THE DISTANCE RUNNERS

In both cases, Stephen would get there first. The reasoning is simple. Suppose it takes one hour to cover the distance. When Charles reaches the halfway mark, Stephen will still keep running and can never be caught up with. If they start walking, the same applies, as it is simply the first race run in reverse. Needless to say, the result is the same irrespective of time and distance.

The key to the solution is that you run further in half the time than half the distance.

66. TWO WALL CLOCKS

1. In 720 days. The clocks will show the same time when the gain of the kitchen clock plus the loss of my father's clock equals 43,200 seconds (12 hours), i.e. when $2^1/_2$ seconds amount to 12 hours, which will be in 720 days.
2. In 3,600 days. The clocks will show the correct time when my clock is a multiple of 12 hours fast and my father's clock is a multiple of 12 hours slow. This will happen to me every 43,200 hours, equal to 1,800 days, and to my father every 1,200 days. The lowest common multiple of the two is 3,600 days.

67. THE APPLICANTS

Andrew knew that he must be wearing a white hat. Had he been wearing a black hat, David would have immediately known that he, David, had to be wearing a white one.

68. THE PICNIC

"Trial and error" will yield the answer eventually, but there is a quicker way:

Let x be the cost of the sandwiches, and y the cost of the wine; then:

The net cost to Tom and Mary is

$y = 4x$ and $(y + x - 5)$

A third of the cost must be Jonathan's contribution:

$$\frac{y + x - 5}{3} = 5$$

or

$$y + x = 20$$

As $y = 4x$, the sandwiches must have cost £4 and the wine £16.

69. BALANCE THE SCALE

The answer is six. To work it out:

1. Double the load on Figure 1.

2. Three black squares replace the two white squares.

3. Add three triangles on each side.

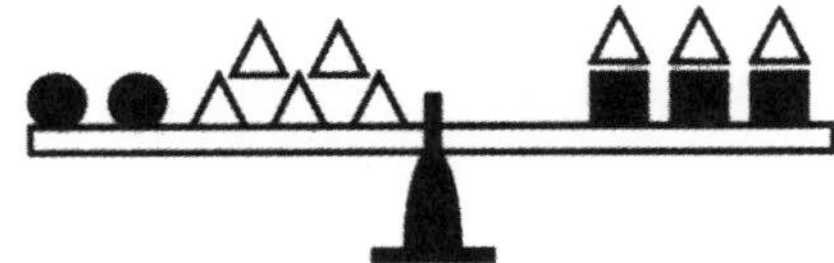

4. Replace each pair of black square and triangle with a circle.

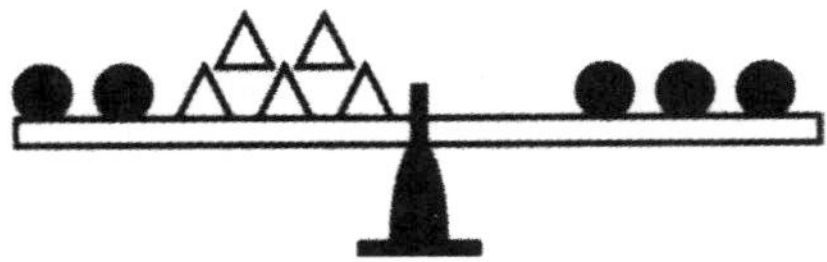

5. Remove two circles on each side for the balance.

70. THE COUNTERFEIT COIN

Two weighings will do it. Put three coins on each of the pans. If they don't balance, take two coins from the lighter side and weigh them. The lighter coin is the fake. If, however, they balance, it is the third coin.

Now let us assume that the three coins on each side balance. Then you proceed with the remaining three as described above.

71. THE WHIPLASH

If the crack is loud enough, it is likely to be the sonic boom caused by the tip exceeding the speed of sound.

72. HIDE AND SEEK

Yes. Even though Evelyne is always facing Tony, with the tree between them, he actually circles everything between himself and the tree.

73. THE WALK TO MARBELLA

A total of 18 miles per hour on average.

Let x be the average speed of the buses. Then:

$$(x + 2) : 50 = (x - 2) : 40$$

or

$$50(x - 2) = 40(x + 2)$$

This reduces to $x = 18$.

74. DROPPING A BRICK

I have to apologize for this trick question. The brick would not sink at all in the vessel at 30° F as the water would be frozen.

However, generally speaking, a brick would sink more slowly in water of lower temperature in view of the higher density of cold water.

75. THE BRIDGE

The truck would have used fuel in travelling over the bridge in excess of the pigeon's weight.

76. SHATTER A WINE GLASS

Depending on the thickness and size, a glass will oscillate at a certain frequency. If the singer hits a note at the same frequency, the oscillations in the glass will build up to a critical point, when it will crack.

77. WHAT'S THE TIME?

It's 2 p.m. The halfway mark between 4 a.m. and 4 p.m. is 10 a.m. That was four hours ago. Therefore, it is now 2 p.m.

78. DECIPHER THE CODE

The message reads THE APPIAN WAY WAS A ROMAN ROAD. (Letters in alphabetical sequence start at A and work left to right, right to left, up the grid.)

The clue was the fifteenth grid. The only two words in the English language that consist of only one letter are "a" and "I".

79. THE PARTY

We are speaking of your right elbow.

80. THE I.Q. TESTS

Sudsic found an easy solution. The average IQ in class "A" was 132, in class "B" 125, and in class "C" 118.

Sudsic's recommendation was to transfer one student from class "A" with an IQ of 130 to class "B", and one student with an IQ of 120 from class "B" to class "C". This simple arrangement raised the average IQ score in each class.

81. A NUMBER RIDDLE

By turning the 9 to make a 6, both columns add up to 21.

82. THE STEEL PLATE

It's 25 revolutions. The barrels are moving forward 2 metres with every revolution, but the plate is, in addition, moving forward 2 metres in respect to the barrels.

83. COMPLETE THE SET

The squares spell . . .	ONE
The triangles spell . . .	TWO
The circles spell . . .	THREE
The ellipses spell . . .	FOUR

Therefore the missing letter is an E.

84. THE DATE

Hugo arrived at 4:40 p.m. and Lynn at 5:25 p.m., when Hugo was no longer waiting.

85. THE RECIPE

Take the following steps:

Tip the glass over a container (Cl) until the milk just reaches the lip of the glass from the edge of the base, as shown in 1 below.

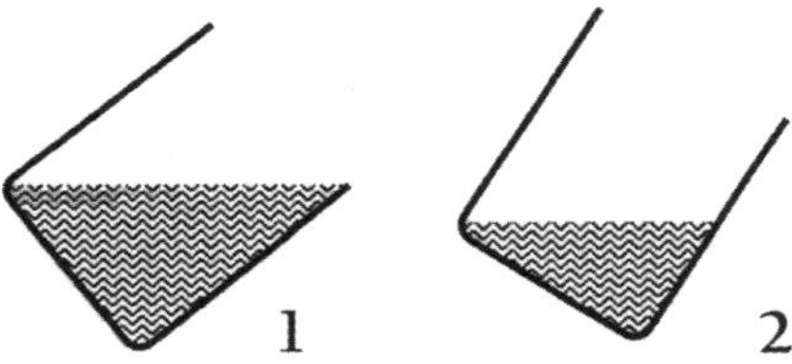

Stand the glass upright; it now contains half a glass of milk. Mark the top level with adhesive tape. Now tilt the glass again, pouring milk out a bit at a time into another container (C2) until it reaches the tape marker, illustration 2. The milk in containers Cl and C2 together is three-quarters of the glass of milk.

86. GEARS

Gear C will make 1,015 revolutions. The other gears will rotate as follows: A 280; B 580; D 1,624; and E 3,248. The lowest common multiple is 32,480 teeth passing the same lowest point.

87. STRANGE SITUATION

The Japanese are husband and wife, both blind from birth.

88. AMBIGUOUS

It is borrow. All the other words can be used as nouns as well as verbs.

89. CARD GAMES

One friend does not play any of the three games but a different card game. The other two must therefore play all games.

90. THE JEWELLERY SHOP

Martin Green went to an auction of surplus police equipment and bought an old police motorcycle with all the usual trappings, upright aerial, etc. He parked it outside his shop and he never had another robbery.

91. IDIOT SAVANT

Total: 1,500,000. The first and tenth, second and ninth, and third and eighth numbers, etc., always add up to 300,000, five times.

92. THE BOARD MEETING

Eleven directors attended. The total number of pages, 169, is only divisible by 1, 13 and 169. For obvious reasons, only 13 copies qualify: eleven directors, the chairman, plus one for the file.

93. THE PC PROBLEM

The keyboard is faulty and prints the next character to the right of, or the first letter in the line below, the one pressed. The coded part of the message reads:

If you solve it, you can keep the PC I lent you. Best regards David

The clue in the letter is cam instead of can.

94. THE LARGE FAMILY

Angela was Lisa's mother. All the other grandchildren were boys.

95. A PAIR OF SOCKS

Three. If I pick three socks, then either they are all of the same colour (in which case I certainly have a pair of the same colour) or else two are of one colour and the third is of the other colour, so in that case I would again have a matching pair.

96. HAIR

The answer to the first question is yes. Assume there are exactly one million people living in Dublin. If each inhabitant had a different number of hairs, then there would be one million different positive whole numbers each less than one million—which is impossible.

The answer to the second problem is 450. Assuming that one islander is completely bald, there are 450 variants between 0 and 449 hairs; but, since we know that no islander has 450 hairs, from 451 hairs onwards the number of variants is the same as the maximum number of hairs, which means that the third fact stated in the question would not hold good for any number of inhabitants higher than 450.

97. THE CLOCK-WATCHER

When George left his house, he started the clock and wrote down the time it then showed. When he got to his sister's house he noted the time when he arrived and the time when he left. He thus knew how long he was at his sister's house. When he got back home, he looked at the clock, so he knew how long he had been away from home. Subtracting from this the time he had spent at his sister's house, he knew how long the walk back and forth had been. By adding half of this to the time he left his sister's house, he then knew what time it really was now.

98. THE PRISONERS' TEST

The man is wearing a red hat. His reasoning is as follows: "The first man did not see 2 white hats. If he had, he would have known immediately that he was wearing a red hat because there are only 2 white hats. The second man, aware that the first did not see 2 white hats, needed only to look at me; if he saw a white hat on me, he would know he was wearing a red hat (otherwise the first man would not have been stumped). Since he didn't know, he could not have seen a white hat on me. Therefore, my hat must be red."

99. ABOVE OR BELOW

The Z goes above the line. The pattern is so simple that many intelligent people miss it: letters consisting of straight lines go above, letters with curves go below!

100. STRANGE SYMBOLS

Alice realized that, behind a looking glass, everything is reflected. The symbols stand for the numbers, one to seven. The right-hand side of each symbol is the correct numeral, the left-hand side is its mirror image. The next symbol in the sequence, then, is a back-to-back figure 8.

101. PRODUCT

Since one of the terms in this series will be $(x - x)$, which equals zero, the product of the entire series is zero.

102. WHAT ARE THEY?

House numbers.

103. MENDING THE CHAIN

The jeweller cut all 3 links on one of the pieces, then used the broken links to join the other segments. He charged £6.

104. FAST FLY

At first glance it may seem that a horrendous calculation is necessary to solve this: the sum of an infinite series of numbers that get smaller and smaller as the cars approach each other. But if you focus on time rather than distance, a solution is easy. The cars are 50 miles apart and traveling towards each other at a combined speed of 50 miles per hour, so they will meet in one hour. In that hour, a fly that flies at 100 miles per hour will naturally travel 100 miles.

105. HOW FAST?

Speedy will have to drive at an infinite speed in order to average 100 miles per hour for the course. He must drive the whole 1,000 miles in 10 hours to attain the required speed, but he has already used up his 10 hours to drive the first half of the course. He will have to finish the race in zero time!

106. WHICH COFFEEPOT?

If these are typical coffeepots, they will both hold the same amount. A pot can be filled only to the level of its spout, otherwise the coffee will spill out. The spouts on both pots rise to the same height.

But these pots may not be typical. If they have hollow handles, as the drawing suggests, the smaller pot would hold more coffee because its entire handle is below the spout line.

107. COCKTAIL

You can do it by moving only two toothpicks. Slide the horizontal one over half a length, then bring down one of the vertical toothpicks to complete the upside-down glass.

108. THE EXPLORER AND THE BEAR

The starting point could be anywhere on a circle drawn around the South Pole at a distance slightly more than 1 x JIT miles (about 1.16

miles) from the Pole. The distance has to be slightly more to take into account the curvature of the Earth. After you have walked a mile south, walking 1 mile east will take you on a complete circuit around the Pole. Finally, walking 1 mile north will return you to your starting point. Thus the starting point could be any one of the infinite number of points on the circle with a radius of about 1.16 miles from the South Pole. However, you could also start at points closer to the Pole, so that the walk east would take you exactly twice around the Pole, or three times, or four times, etc. (though, of course, if you started from any point closer to the Pole than a mile away, the direction of the initial stretch of one mile south would make you reach the Pole, after which you would actually be walking due north "up" the other side).

109. BUTTONS AND BOXES

You can ascertain the contents of all three boxes by taking out just one button.

The solution depends on the fact that the labels on all three boxes are incorrect.

Take a button from the box labeled RG. Assume that the button removed is red. You now know that the other button in this box must be red also, otherwise the label would be correct. Since you have identified which box contains 2 red buttons, you can work out immediately the contents of the box marked GG because you know it cannot contain 2 green buttons since its label has to be wrong. It cannot contain 2 red buttons, for you have already identified that box.

Therefore it must contain one red and one green button. The third box, of course, must then be the one with the 2 green buttons. The same reasoning works if the first button you take from the RG box happens to be green instead of red.

110. MANHATTAN AND YONKERS

Although the trains to Yonkers and Manhattan arrive equally often—every 10 minutes—it so happens that the Manhattan train always arrives one minute after the Yonkers train. Thus, the Manhattan train will be the first to arrive only if Amy happens to arrive at the station during this 1-minute interval. If she enters the station at any other time, during the 9-minute interval, the Yonkers train will arrive first. Since Amy's arrival is random, the odds are 9 to 1 in favour of Yonkers.

111. COUNTERFEIT COINS

Only a single weighing is necessary to identify the counterfeit stack. Let x be the weight of a genuine silver dollar. Take 1 coin from stack No. 1, 2 from stack No. 2, 3 from stack No. 3, and so on to the entire 10 coins from stack No. 10. Weigh the whole sample.

The sample should weigh 55x. The number of grams over or under 55x the sample weighs corresponds to the number of the stack containing the counterfeit coins. For instance, if the sample weighs 7 grams more than it should (or 7 grams less), then the stack containing the counterfeit coins is No. 7.

112. FAKE!

The point of this puzzle is that the counterfeit coin has to be identified in a limited number of weighings even though, at the outset, we do not know whether the counterfeit is heavier or lighter than a genuine coin.

The key to solving it lies in the fact that, as the first and second weighings narrow the field, we learn that certain coins can only be either genuine or light (but not heavy), and certain others can only be genuine or heavy.

In the following explanation it is assumed that, whenever a weighing reveals an imbalance, it is the left scale that is heavy. Of course, the right scale is just as likely to be heavier, but this does not affect the reasoning; it simply reverses the conclusions to be drawn about the coins in each scale. Coins proven to be genuine are designated by the symbol *x*.

1. Weigh coins 1, 2, 3,4 against coins 5, 6, 7, 8.

If:

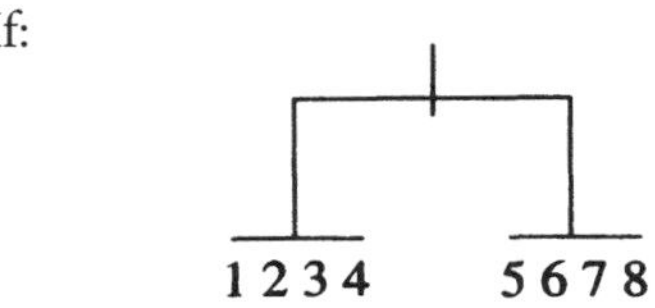

2. Weigh coins 9, 10 against coins 11, *x* (*x* being any of coins 1-8).

If:

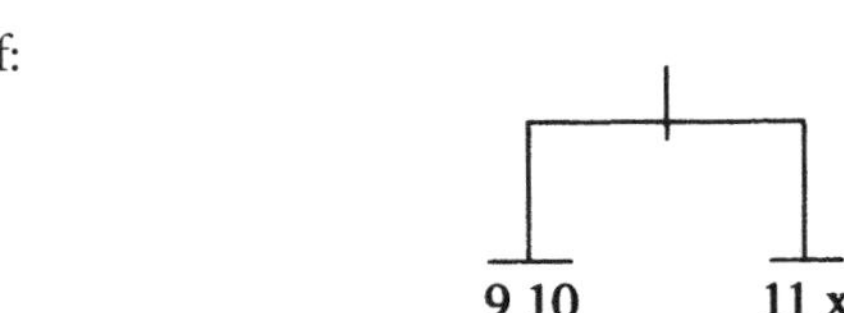

Coin 12 is the counterfeit. (A third weighing would determine whether it is heavy or light.)

If:

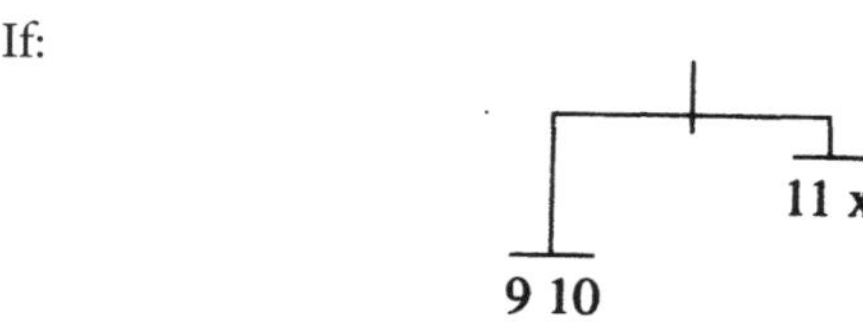

Then, obviously, the counterfeit is either 9, 10 or 11. In the example shown, we can tell that either 9 or 10 is heavy, or 11 is light. (Similarly, if the scale were reversed, we would know for certain that either 9 or 10 is light, or 11 is heavy.)

3. Weigh coins 10, 11 against x, x. If they balance, 9 is the counterfeit (and we know whether it is light or heavy depending on the result of the second weighing). If they do not balance, then 10 or 11 must be the counterfeit coin, and we can determine which by comparing the result of the second weighing with that of the third.

If:

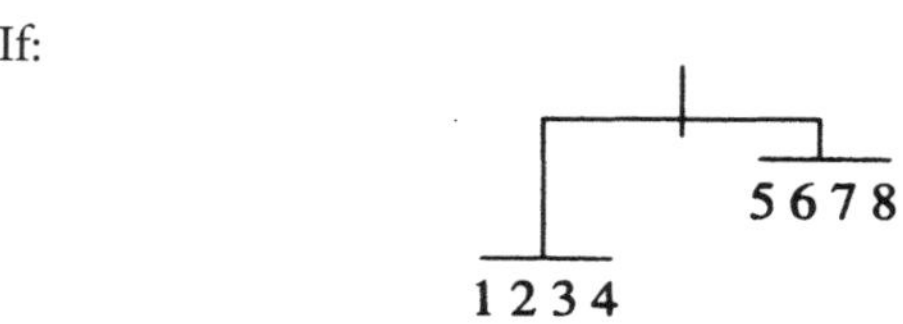

We know that coins 9-12 are genuine. Also that either one of 1, 2, 3 and 4 is heavy, or one of 5, 6, 7 and 8 is light.

4. Weigh coins 1, 5, x against 2, 6, 7.

If:

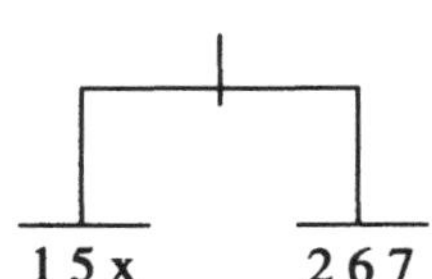

Then we know either 3 or 4 is heavy, or 8 is light.

5. Weigh coin 3 against 4.
If they balance, coin 8 is the counterfeit and it is light. If they do not balance, whichever is the heavier is the counterfeit.

If:

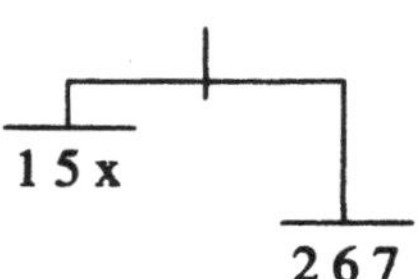

Then we know either 1 is heavy, or 6 or 1 is light.

6. Weigh coin 6 against 7.
If they balance, coin 1 is the counterfeit and it is heavy. If they do not balance, the lighter is the counterfeit.

If:

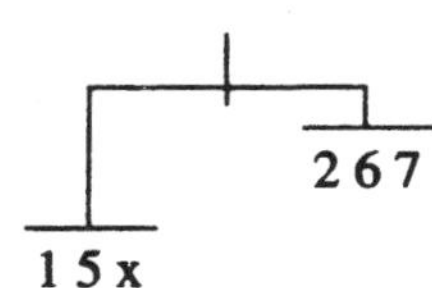

Then either 5 is light or 2 is heavy (the only explanations for the imbalance switching).

7. Weigh either coin 5 or coin 2 against x to determine which is the counterfeit coin.

113. HOW LONG?

19.2 metres.

Let x be the length of the bolt. Then $\frac{x}{3} + \frac{x}{4} + 8 = x$. This reduces to:

$$4x + 3x + 96 = 12x, \text{ or } 5x = 96$$

$\therefore x = 19.2$ metres.

114. ARITHMETIC PROBLEM

Ten problems.

Let x be the number of correct solutions, and y be the number of incorrect solutions.

Then: $x + y = 26$

and $8x - 5y = 0$

From first equation $y = (26 - x)$

$\therefore \quad 8x - 5(26 - x) = 0$

or $8x = 130 - 5x$

$\therefore \quad x = 10$

115. THE CLOAK

x = value of the coat. After seven months the butler is entitled to $^{7x}/_{12} + ^{700}/_{12}$. However, he receives only £20, therefore, $^{5x}/_{12}$ must compensate for the difference between £$^{700}/_{12}$ and £$^{240}/_{12}$ (£20)

therefore, $5x = 460$

and $x = £92$

116. WATERLILIES

As in fact you are starting with two waterlilies on the second day, you save one day, therefore the answer is 29 days.

117. TWO STEAMERS

The second, because

$$\frac{x}{30} + \frac{x}{40}$$

is greater than

$$\frac{2x}{35}$$

Proof:

$$\frac{x}{30} + \frac{x}{40} = \frac{7x}{120} \text{ or } \frac{245x}{4200}$$

$$\frac{2x}{35} = \frac{240x}{4200}$$

118. UNEQUAL SCALES

It depends on the reason for the scales' imbalance. If the pans are of unequal weights, the grocer's solution will work; but if the arms of the scale are of unequal lengths, it will not, and the grocer will lose.

119. THE LONG DIVISION

First, observe that the five-digit quotient forms only three products with the divisor. Therefore, two of the five digits must be zeros. These cannot be the first or last, since both obviously form products. They are therefore the second and fourth digits, those covered by the white Bishops. Furthermore, the two-digit divisor, when multiplied by 8, gives a two-digit product; but when multiplied by another number, the one concealed under the first white Rook, it gives a three-digit product; the multiplier hidden under the first white Rook must therefore be larger than 8, namely 9. Both the first and last digits in the quotient give three-digit products with the two-digit divisor; both must therefore be 9. We now have established the quotient: it is 90,809. Let us find the divisor, covered up beneath the two white Knights. When multiplied by 8 it forms a two-digit product; when multiplied by 9 it forms a three-digit product. It must, therefore, be 12; $8 \times 12 = 96$, $9 \times 12 = 108$; neither 10, 11, 13 nor any larger number meets these requirements. The numbers under the remaining chess pieces are now readily ascertainable.

120. TWO BOLTS

The bolt heads will remain at the same distance from each other in both cases.

Assume that bolt A has not a thread but parallel rings and you swing bolt B around it. The heads will approach or move away, depending on whether you swing counter- or clockwise. As, however, bolt A has the same thread as B they cancel each other out.

Another explanation:

If instead of swinging bolt B around bolt A, you leave B in situ but turn it clockwise, then the heads will approach. Indeed this is the function of a screw, as bolt "A" can be considered a nut. If you turn B anticlockwise, you "unscrew" and the heads will move away. However if you do neither but just swing B around then the heads will remain where they are.

121. SURVIVING A DUEL

The poorest shot, the Baron of Rockall, has the best chance of surviving. Lord Montcrief, the one who never misses, has the second best chance. Because the Baron's two opponents will aim at each other when their turns come, his best strategy is to fire into the air until one of the others is killed. He will then get the first shot at the survivor, which gives him the advantage.

122. FAIR SHARES

There are several possible solutions. However, the following method has the advantage of leaving no excess pieces of cake.

Assume 4 people are sharing the cake. Call them A, B, C and D. First, A cuts off what he is content to keep as his $^1/_4$ of the cake. Next B has the option, if he thinks A's slice is more than $^1/_4$, of reducing it by cutting off some of it. If B thinks A's slice is $^1/_4$ or less, he does nothing. C and D in turn then have an opportunity to do the same with A's slice. The last person to touch this slice keeps it as his share. If anyone thinks that this last person has less than $^1/_4$ he is naturally pleased because it means, in his eyes, that more than $^1/_4$ remains. The remainder of the cake, including any cut-off pieces, is now divided among the remaining 3 persons in the same manner, then among 2. The final division is made by one person doing the cutting and the other the choosing. This procedure can be applied to any number of persons.

123. RACING DRIVER

160 miles per hour. The key lies in converting miles per hour to miles per minute and in using fractions instead of decimals to avoid rounding errors.

Using the formula Time (T) = $\frac{\text{Distance (D)}}{\text{Speed(S)}}$

If driver travels 3 miles at 140 miles per hour, it takes him $^9/_7$ minutes to cover the distance.

Equally, $1^1/_2$ miles at 168 miles per hour will take $^{15}/_{28}$ minutes and $1^1/_2$ miles at 210 miles per hour takes $^3/_7$ minutes.

$\therefore$ Total time for six miles $= \frac{9}{7} + \frac{15}{28} + \frac{3}{7}$ minutes.

This reduces to $\frac{63}{28}$ minutes for 6 miles.

Using above formula $S = \frac{D}{T} = \frac{6 \times 28}{63}$ per minute

or: $\frac{6 \times 28 \times 60}{63}$ per hour

This reduces to 160 miles per hour.

124. THE SIDE VIEW

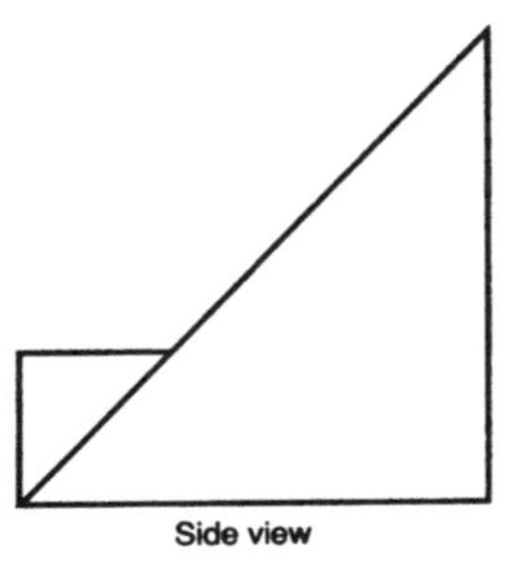
Side view

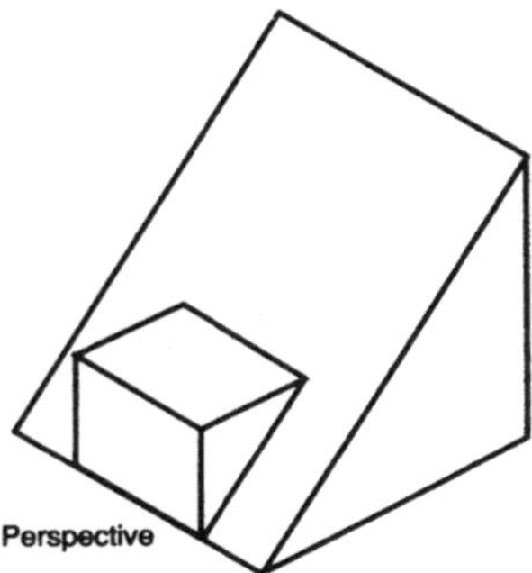
Perspective

FALLACIES AND PARADOXES

125. THE ODDS

Dick should not accept, as the odds are very unfavourable. When you remove one card from the group of three, the probability that the Joker will be your card is one in three, and the probability that it will be one of the two left on the table is two in three. However, since it is certain that one of the cards left on the table is an ace, the odds are not altered by Tom turning the ace over, which means that the odds of the card left face down on the table being the Joker are still two in three.

126. THE DICE

Galileo observed that the six combinations were not equally likely. For instance, 3 + 3 + 3 to yield 9 can arise only in one way, namely when each of the dice displays a 3. On the other hand, all the combinations yielding 10 can arise in several ways. For instance, 2 + 4 + 4 can arise in three ways, because the 2 can come from any of the three dice.

127. THE THREE-COIN FALLACY

It is fallacious to assume that the third coin can have only two positions, i.e. heads or tails. This would apply only if the third coin were always the same. In fact, three coins can give rise to the following permutations:

H H H
H H T
H T H
H T T
T H H
T T H
T H T
T T T

This proves that the probability that all coins come out alike, i.e. H H H or T T T, is indeed 2 in 8, or 1/4.

128. ZENO'S PARADOX OR ACHILLES AND THE TORTOISE

Zeno's argument would stand up only for a limited distance, in fact for one less than 1,111.9 metres, at which distance the race would be a tie. For a shorter distance, the tortoise would win; for a longer one, the victor would be Achilles.

129. THE ROULETTE FALLACY

The snag is that a card deck consists of twenty-six red and twenty-six black cards while, at the roulette table, the two colours, even in medium runs, do not appear equally often. Consequently, in unbalanced runs you could lose much more than you could win. Casinos in Monte Carlo keep records from which it appears that runs of ten and more in one colour are not infrequent.

130. THE MARBLE PARADOX

No! We have four marbles:

White (W)
Yellow (Y)
Blue (Bl)
Blue (B2)

You have the following six possibilities of drawing two marbles:

W-Y	Y-Bl	B1-B2
W-Bl	Y-B2	
W-B2		

W-Y is eliminated, but all the other five draws will produce a blue marble. Therefore, the correct solution is one in five.

131. THE SERIES PARADOX

The series can be shown as:

$$(6 - 6) + (6 - 6) + (6 - 6) + (6 - 6) + 6 = 6$$

or $$(6 - 6) + (6 - 6) + (6 - 6) + (6 - 6) = 0$$

The answer is alternatively 0 and 6 forever. Therefore, the minimum value is $^1/_6$ and the maximum is $^1/_0$, which is ∞.

132. THE SEVERED ARM

The nine men, including John, were shipwrecked together on a remote, uninhabited island in the South Pacific during the Second World War.

Their only hope of rescue was a search operation by the US Air Force or Navy. As the days passed and their rations ran out, they faced a hard choice between dying one by one or cannibalizing parts of their bodies. They agreed on the latter course, beginning by sacrificing their left forearms. They drew straws to determine in what order they would have their limbs severed, but first they swore a pact that, should they be rescued before they had each had an arm removed, those in the group remaining whole would make arrangements to have their left arms amputated later.

The group was rescued after 8 of the 9 men had had an arm severed. The war ended shortly afterwards. Once back in the civilian world, John quickly thought better of his promise, and hit upon a scheme to deceive his comrades into believing he had honoured the pact.

133. THE LIFT STOPPED

The woman's husband depends on a life support system connected to the electricity supply in their flat on the tenth floor. What happened to the lift made the woman realize the building was suffering a power failure.

134. THE BARBER SHOP

David and the barber's wife are having an affair. They arrange their meetings for the end of the day, and David checks on the barber's workload to make sure he won't be home too soon.

135. THE CAR CRASH

Shame on you, you male chauvinist! The surgeon was Mrs.-er, Ms.—Jones, Robert's mother.

136. A GLASS OF WATER

The man had hiccups. The bartender's action, producing a sudden shock, was a quicker-acting cure than a glass of water might have been.

137. THE UNFAITHFUL WIFE

On Eva's way out, Charles had noticed a run in her left stocking. When she went to the kitchen for coffee, he noticed that the run was on her right leg.

138. THE SUICIDE

Plod wasted his last years. The husband was completely innocent. The heiress had committed suicide by tying a noose around her neck, standing on a block of ice and kicking the ice out from under her. It had fallen into the bath (or Jacuzzi) and melted overnight while her husband was away.

139. THE DEADLY SCOTCH

The poison was inside the ice cubes, which dissolved in Lay's drink, but not in El's.

140. THE TWO ACCOUNTANTS

Fred Jones and Helen Smith were lovers, Smith having deceived Jones into believing she was single and interested in marriage.

141. THE ANTIQUE CANDELABRUM

The elderly man had mentioned to the dealer that the candelabrum was one of a rare pair that together were worth much more than twice the value of the one; the man told the dealer he had been looking for the pair for many years. He bought the one candelabrum for £5,000, making it clear that he would pay handsomely if the dealer would locate its twin.

Not realizing that the elderly man was a confidence trickster, the dealer then called around some of his friends in the trade until he was tipped off about a collector who was offering to sell a candelabrum just like the one the dealer had sold to the elderly man.

Triumphantly, the dealer tracked down this "second" candelabrum to Robert, and agreed to buy it from him for £9,000, expecting to make a killing when he sold it on to the elderly man as the second part of the complete pair. Needless to say, the elderly man disappeared without trace but *with* £4,000 profit!

142. THE LIFT JOCKEY

Bill walks up eight floors, not by choice but because he is only four feet six inches tall, and cannot reach higher than the fifteenth floor on the lift's button panel. Whenever he has company in the lift, he asks someone to press 23 for him.

143. THE CROSSROADS

George, somewhat piqued, asked her: "Aren't you going to drink?" "Not until the police have been here," she replied, removing the bottle and glasses.

VISUAL-SPATIAL TEST

144. A, F.
145. D, F.
146. D. (All the others can be rotated into each other.)
147. E.
148. C.
149. C. (A and B, as well as D and E respectively, can be rotated into each other.)
150. 9. (The circles are halved with horizontal, vertical or diagonal lines, and are shaded white or black. The dividing line in 9 should be horizontal.)
151. C. (The clock shows 3, 6, 9 and 12 o'clock. The C position does not exist.)
152. 3. (The symbols move clockwise, and the black dot is situated between the cross and the circle except in 3.)
153. E. (The black top segment moves one step clockwise; the bottom segment moves two steps anticlockwise.)
154. D. (All the others can be rotated into each other.)
155. B. (All the other shapes are symmetrical about a horizontal and a vertical line.)
156. 4, 6, 7. (The other four can be rotated into each other.)
157. C. (We have a cab, two wheels and a coupling. The black wheel is always to the right of the white wheel and to the left of the shaded wheel. The cab is shaded from the left to upper right except when

there are shaded wheels, when it is reversed. The coupling is either black, white or shaded, differing from the wheels.)

158. 4. (Each row is the mirror image of the row underneath, including the shading.)
159. E. (The third column contains lines which columns one and two have in common.)
160. C. (Each triangle above the line counts plus one, below the line minus one. The last column is the addition/subtraction.)
161. E. (The triangle like the square is turned 45°, and the letter J becomes the mirror image.)
162. E. (The sine curve becomes a straight line, and the square is stretched to become a rectangle.)
163. D. (The order in which the letters are rearranged is 4231.)
164. B. (The shape is turned 180°.)
165. B. (The rectangle becomes an extended line, the line becomes a rectangle. The same applies to the rectangle on the triangle.)
166. C. (The shaded sector moves anticlockwise, the black sector clockwise.)
167. A and E.
168. A and D.
169. 4. (The right angle is moving anticlockwise. The changing figure increases the number of its line segments by one in each succeeding square.)
170. 5 and 6. (The triangle is turned through an angle of 90° anti-clockwise. Forms 5 and 6 do not match.)
171. A-C and B-D-E.

172. 1, 6. (They are vertically and horizontally symmetrical, the others only vertically.)
173. F (The lines in the top row increase from 3 to 6, followed by 7.)
174. 3. (There are three shapes of ears, shadings of bodies and bases; each occurs only once in each row.)
175. C. (Dots on the left are counted plus, on the right side minus. The series runs 6, 5, 4, 3, 2, with C being 1.)
176. The white circle and the black triangle move anticlockwise, the black circle moves clockwise.
177. 2 and 6. (All the others are Roman numerals.)

PUZZLE NOTES

PUZZLE NOTES

PUZZLE NOTES